— *The* —

FATHER'S

GUIDE *to the*

MEANING *of* LIFE

WHAT BEING A DAD HAS TAUGHT ME
ABOUT HOPE, LOVE, PATIENCE, PRIDE,
AND EVERYDAY WONDER

BY JOE KITA

AUTHOR OF *WISDOM OF OUR FATHERS*
EXECUTIVE WRITER, **Men'sHealth** MAGAZINE

DAYBREAK

Cover Series Designer: Lee Fukui
Cover Designer: Stephanie M. Tarone
Interior Designer: Susan P. Eugster
Cover Illustrator: Nip Rogers

Library of Congress Cataloging-in-Publication Data

Kita, Joe.
     The father's guide to the meaning of life : what being a dad has
  taught me about hope, love, patience, pride, and everyday wonder /
  by Joe Kita.
          p.   cm.
     ISBN 1–57954–289–1 hardcover
     1. Fatherhood—Psychological aspects.   I. Title.
  HQ756 .K58   2000
  306.874'2—dc21   00–026354

Distributed to the book trade by St. Martin's Press

2   4   6   8   10   9   7   5   3   1   hardcover

Visit us on the Web at www.rodalebooks.com,
or call us toll-free at (800) 848-4735.

Contents

Acknowledgments

Most parents look at raising children as a top-down process. The father, the mother, the schools, the son, the daughter. And the product, after many years of shaping, is a polished young adult. But suppose we turn this process upside-down? Suppose that when a child is born, we don't automatically assume our job is solely to raise it or (let's be honest) change it? Suppose we decide to let this baby girl or boy, this already perfect being, raise us? As we help them grow up, so they will help us mature. As we teach them the rules of life, so they will show us its deeper meaning.

That's the simple journey of this book. I've re-visited 15 unique experiences I've had over the years with my two kids, and then considered what each one taught me about life and myself. The more I wrote, the more amazed I became. My children have been incredible educators. They have taught me so much I hadn't even realized, so much I had incorporated into my life without knowing where it came from. Whereas parents assume it's their children who should be eternally grateful to them, it's really us who should be thankful to our kids. They make us whole in ways we hardly know.

So maybe for the first time, I'd like to thank my children, Paul and Claire, for teaching me more than I ever expected and for changing me in ways I never anticipated. And thanks to my beautiful wife, Maria, whose assistance, of course, made it all possible. And thanks also to my father, whose sudden death started me thinking about the meaning of life. He goes on teaching me. But now I have the satisfaction, however small, of knowing I at least returned the favor.

lesson one

Play

For my son's second birthday, I bought him Rock 'em, Sock 'em Robots. In case you never lusted after this game as a child, it features two brawny machine-men inside a miniature boxing ring. Each player uses hand controls to maneuver his robot while thumbing buttons to throw left and right uppercuts. When you hit your opponent's jaw in just the right place, there's a satisfying *"Eeeyyyaaawww"* sound as his head springs up. This is called knocking his block off.

It's that simple. It's that thrilling.

Indeed, I am so excited by this gift, I'm barely able to resist helping my son unwrap it. "It's Rock 'em,

1

Sock 'em Robots!" I scream, since he obviously doesn't know what it is. But the box is big and colorful, and that's exciting enough. While he smacks the tray of his high chair in delight, I begin assembly.

"Don't you think he's a little young for that?" asks my wife.

"Oh no, dear," I reply, weaving the ring ropes through the plastic turnbuckles. "He's going to love it. It's a classic! I always wanted one when I was a kid."

"But it's so violent. Suppose he tries knocking somebody's block off at day care?"

"Aw come on. It's harmless. Here, I'll show you."

And with that, I place the game reverently between my son and me. He leans forward attentively as I demonstrate how to throw punches and glide around the ring. Then we touch gloves, I yell "Ding! Ding!" and the fighting commences.

For a while, it's mayhem. He comes out of his corner, flailing and squealing. I cover up. Then, as his little thumbs begin to tire, I respond with a flurry of brutal right uppercuts. One finally hits home, and his block gets knocked off. (*Eeeyyyaaawww!*) I jab the air in jubilation, and my son starts to cry.

"It's okay, it's okay. Look, we can pop the robot's head right back on. See?"

After he realizes that defeat is temporary, he calms down, we regroup in our respective corners, and we emerge to battle again and again.

Since then, as my son has grown, I've had similar bouts of joy with radio-controlled cars, Nerf guns, model trains, Creepy Crawlers, and whole battalions of little green army men. I used to love to wander the aisles at Toys 'R' Us with a shopping cart, throwing in all those things I begged for as a kid but my parents refused to buy. It was power, it was freedom, it was the essence of independent adulthood.

But even more delightful than the purchasing was the playing: sitting Indian-style on the floor with my son, surrounded by 750 individual pieces from a giant Lego pirate ship, breath heavy with concentration, time suspended. I was never happier, never more relaxed, than when I finally pushed aside the work in my day and agreed to play.

Why was that?

I think part of the reason is because play is in-stinctual. You see it in cubs; you see it in kids. Give a child an interesting object, and it follows as natu-rally as giggles from a tickle. It is how we learn, how we explore, how we first open our minds. And when we stumble across it as adults, part of us remembers this and prepares to grow again. The older we get, the more exciting that possibility is.

Another reason is that play provides balance. It's a built-in buffer to stress, a sort of conscious version of sleep. Think about it. What rest does passively for us at night, play achieves actively for us during the day. It's restorative. It's refreshing. It's another subtle dimension of life from which we awaken slightly better. For proof, watch children coloring, or listen to the happy hum of a school yard at recess. The de-light in the moment is utter and pure. Play is child's meditation, a toddler's trance, the most tender Zen.

But adults don't appreciate this. Most times we are too busy to play, too mature to get down there on the floor. When our children implore us, we give in grudgingly and then remain distracted by the hive of priorities in our lives. We place such little value on play that we can rarely immerse ourselves in it guiltlessly.

Yet some stubborn part of us continues to insist upon it, like nourishment for a starving part of the psyche. So we search out new, more adult ways to play, without ever realizing what we're pursuing or even what we need. What is a fitness club but a big chrome playground? Only instead of having fun inside, we quantify all our motion, call it *working* out, and eventually drop out. What is a bedroom but our own private amusement park? Only instead of being honest and free with our partner, we often handcuff ourselves with insecurity. And what is a hobby but a brand new toy? Only instead of focusing on its simple inherent joy, we let it get so high-tech that our level of satisfaction is determined financially.

The 68-year-old writer Wilfrid Sheed told me this when I asked him for the secret to happiness: "Develop something outside of yourself," he said, "a burning interest in Napoleon or the Civil War or anything that inspires the same kind of passion that kids have with ease but adults somehow forget about. I've never known an unhappy person with a stamp collection."

He was referring, of course, to play. In fact, I thought I saw him the other day, behind a buggy and a big grin at Toys 'R' Us. The point is that the thrill of getting a new bike is no less grand at 75 than it is at 5. It still feels just as good now to swing a bat, throw a Frisbee, run fast, or do a waterhole cannonball as it did then. It has to do with a willingness to call time out for recess and then be unafraid to do something spontaneous.

I found the Rock 'em, Sock 'em Robots the other day, deep in the toy closet, long since packed away. I started to get wistful, remembering my son's second birthday and how much fun we had. I started to wish for good old times like that, when life was innocent and uncomplicated and free. And then I stopped myself, realizing that it still is. I opened the box, wove the ring ropes through the plastic turnbuckles, and then set off to find my 14-year-old boy—the one in my house and the one still inside me.

lesson two

Secrets

HOW TO SHARE A PERFECT,

WORDLESS MESSAGE OF LOVE

My daughter and I have a secret handshake. It has evolved over the years into a pretty advanced hand dance that we exchange every night before she goes to bed. It consists of seven distinct moves, ending with the whispered words "Hala Hala Hala." (Neither of us knows what this means, other than that it's a catchy phrase from a Barenaked Ladies song we both like.)

I don't know how this ritual got started, just that we've been doing it for a long time. She added something; then I suggested an even goofier variation. Now the whole thing is delightfully complex

7

and still developing. By the time she's grown, it may take us 10 minutes to say good night instead of the usual 10 seconds. But, no doubt, it'll always make us smile. And that is a beautiful way to put a ribbon around the day and begin dreaming of tomorrow.

Claire would be angry if she knew I had told you even this much. After all, no one—not her brother, not her mother, not even her best friend— is supposed to know the specifics. It is our private code. So I'd appreciate your keeping it a secret.

There's something else I should probably tell you, because it'll help explain why I value this silly handshake so much. But I share it hesitantly, with the same guilty feelings of betrayed trust. Only this time, it's my own confidence I'm breaching.

Ever since I can remember, I've had difficulty showing affection. I've always hesitated before giving a kiss or a hug, actually struggled with the words "I love you." What other people seem to do so naturally with family and friends, I feel awkward about—even with my wife and kids.

I'm not dead inside. I have powerful feelings

that sometimes well up and almost make me cry. Whenever this happens, I rehearse what I'm going to say, what I'll do with these hands, but when the opportunity comes to touch another heart, I rarely can. It feels too sappy, too much like an overworked scene from some classic movie. And I'm no actor.

Like everything else, I guess it stems from my childhood. I honestly can't remember ever seeing my mother and father kiss, embrace, or even hold hands. And I rarely recall having these outward signs of affection bestowed upon me. It's not that there wasn't any love in our family; it's just that the softness in our hearts existed within a shell of self-consciousness.

The lesson I learned is that love is private and that public tokens of it are just that: tokens. That's the virtuous explanation. But I also learned that it's safer to never show your emotions, that you never have to fear exposure if you've never opened up, that those who don't reach out can stop others from reaching in. That's the coward's interpretation—the one I'm most guilty of.

I wrote another book about fatherhood a couple

of years ago. Part of it involved asking men age 50 and older to share their biggest regrets. Among the hundreds of stirring confessions I heard, there was one in particular I'll never forget. It came from an 81-year-old war hero, one of those steel-hard guys with ice-blue eyes who you think will never die. But it turned out he already had, and quite painfully.

"My biggest regret in life was assuming she knew," he said, hanging his head. "I should have told my wife I loved her. I thought she understood that. But she didn't. And that was my mistake. I never said what I should have said. And we got divorced because of it."

This powerful, imposing man was courageous in every way, except where it really counted. I realized then that he was just like me. His purple heart symbolized ache, not true bravery.

By the time I had finished researching that book, I'd met many others: Men who didn't list the expected regrets of fame, money, or success but rather the consistently missed opportunity to show their emotions openly. What was sobering is that

they were decades ahead of me—each having followed the thinning red line of love out to its meager
end. There was no regret more poignant, none that
moved me so much, because it was my future con-
fession I was hearing—the sad epitaph to a life untouched.

That's when I started looking upon our secret
handshake as something more than a good-night
goof. I realize it is my clumsy, immature way of
saying "I love you." And I think my daughter realizes this, too. Like any child, she knows that secrets
are special and that those who share them are naturally close. For her, I hope, it's enough. And for me,
I like to think, it's a start.

I see the same emotionless inclinations in my
14-year-old son, how he mumbles his affection, how
he already thinks he's too big to hug, how he'd
rather shake hands than embrace the whole of you,
how he thinks that's what it takes to be a man.
Funny how they learn.

But this is one instance where I don't want my
boy to be like me, where it hurts to see the imita-

tion. There is no flattery in teaching someone in-sincerity. So the other night, when he was in bed, I went into his room and suggested we start our own secret handshake. Although he was almost asleep, he stirred immediately, held out his hand, and grinned. We've only choreographed two moves so far, but it's early. These things take time.

There's something else I want to share with you. But I'd appreciate your keeping this a secret, too. It's a dream of mine, about how I'd like things to end.

I am old and dying, laid out on some hospital bed. My family has been summoned and, like a classic movie scene, the last rites have been read. It's time for final words, and although I've spent a life-time writing, I'm still having trouble speaking. So I hold out my hand—first to Claire and then to Paul. It has been years, but each of them instantly recalls. Slowly, meaningfully, we exchange our secret hand-shakes. Fingers touching. Hearts, too. And this is how we part—having said it all without having said anything.

And, of course, we are smiling.

THE ESSENTIAL TRAITS
OF A FATHER

Children would have you be perfect. In that sense, every parent is bound to some level of failure. But if you have the following attributes, you will be as good as any father can be.

KNOWLEDGEABLE

A child's inclination is to question the world, and a father's duty is to supply as many answers as he can. This doesn't necessarily take a high degree of intelligence. In fact, you can usually do a pretty good job with just basic common sense. The important thing to remember is that even if you don't know the explanation, your kid thinks you do. Don't let him down. There's no compliment that's greater.

PATIENT

When I was a boy and I did something wrong, I used to run to my father's closet and tie knots in all his belts. That way, when he inevitably reached for one, it would take a while to undo. And in that time, his anger would subside and he'd begin thinking rationally again. A father needs to knot his own belts. He needs patience so he'll hesitate before reprimanding, pause before judging, and wait until the both of you are good and ready.

CURIOUS

Few things unite a dad and his kids more than mutual wonder and the urge to explore. When you get down on your hands and knees, first in amazement at something you see and then in a determined search to unearth a clue, you are becoming your child's equal. It is by learning that we grow wise and also young. Kids are forever asking, "Why?" Good fathers do, too.

GENEROUS

Be generous with your time, your money, your possessions, your love, your soul. If you aren't prepared to completely share every facet of your life and, most important, yourself, then you aren't ready to become a father. Now that my kids are getting older, my life is finally starting to come back. I can call it *my* life again. Whereas for the last decade and a half, it's been *ours*.

IMPERFECT

The best dads are the ones who aren't afraid to screw up in front of their kids. They're the ones who drop an occasional fly ball and laugh, who burn a meal and then treat everyone to dinner, who call a repairman to fix what they couldn't, who finish second (or last) with no regrets. These guys make such good fathers because they're so real. If you're not perfect, your children never feel they have to be.

RESPECTFUL

Have respect for three things: your body, your spouse, and God. Keeping yourself in good shape teaches your children self-esteem. Loving their mother unconditionally shows them that they should too. And humbling yourself before God lets them know that there will always be something bigger than themselves.

LOYAL

No matter how fed up I got with my old man, I knew there was one thing I could count on. He'd always be there to pick me up, just like he said he would, initially by car and then later in life with a good word or a few bucks. I never realized how much that support meant until he died. Your children need to know that, no matter what, your love remains. It'll never be late; it'll never leave early. You are the one person they can depend on.

lesson three

Happiness

It's a rainy Sunday afternoon, and there's nothing to do. My wife has gone to work, so I'm home alone with the kids. "Try to spend some quality time with them," is what she said before she left.

But the remnants of my failed attempts are ankle-deep on the family room floor—a Monopoly board, the bubble from Trouble, hundreds of Legos, spent rows of dominoes, Nintendo cartridges, Lite-Brite pieces. . . . And that smell? It's burnt brownies from the deceptively named E-Z Bake Oven.

My children sit amongst it all with pained

faces, doing their dramatic interpretation of death by boredom. They are both very good actors.

But it's not until my daughter toddles to the toy closet and begins pulling out Barbie and Ken's Fabulous Fashion Runway that I panic. I suggest something so foolish, so dumb, that it immediately makes them smile and cheer. In retrospect, I should have said I was kidding right then and there.

Paul and Claire have been begging for a dog for years. But my wife has remained adamant. "The day you bring an animal into this house is the day I leave," she warned. This scared them at first, but lately they've been weighing the comparative liabilities:

A dog? No mom?

A dog? No mom?

To my wife's concern, their decision has been prolonged.

I want to make it clear, however, that I never intended to actually purchase a dog. My exact words, and I quote, were: "Why don't we go *look* at puppies?" I realize now this is like saying "Let's go look at chocolate candy." What I failed to recognize is that children can't distinguish between browsing and buying. I had somehow forgotten all those spectacular fits at Toys 'R' Us.

So off we drive—filled with excitement and very different expectations. I try to do the noble thing by initially taking them to some animal shelters. At the first, we walk an indifferent shar-pei named Pete. His prior owners had abandoned him not once, not twice, but three times along the freeway. No wonder the only time he looks at us is when he squats to take a crap.

The next shelter is even worse. When we ask to see the dogs, the woman in charge says that won't be possible. "They're not very good with children, but here are some photos. If you see any you like, I can bring them out." We glance at a bunch of sad Polaroids, as out-of-focus as these poor animals' lives, then quickly leave before our guilt gets the better of us. So far, this has been more depressing than fun.

But then we pull up to Jack's Dog Farm, "in business since 1936, just past Ottsville on route

611." It's a big, white barn of a building with a giant statue of a dog guarding the parking lot. Turns out, Jack himself is dead. In charge now is a Saint Bernard of a man named Jeremy. (He pronounces it "Germy.") The guy is so huge, his armpits could double as whelping boxes.

Business is brisk. The office is crowded, the phone is ringing, and Germy is swiping credit cards faster than a Times Square pickpocket. At his invitation, we step inside and stroll the aisles between cages. Large weepy eyes and soft furry faces stare back at us—innocent inmates waiting to be sprung. Naturally, my kids are overcome.

Then it happens. As I'm standing there, smiling naively and congratulating myself on the quality time we're sharing, they spot an 8-week-old Jack Russell terrier just as she spots them. Pink-nosed and completely white, except for brown patches over each eye, she stands on her hind legs and whimpers a greeting.

"Oh! Look at this one!" my daughter says, melting. "She's so-o-o sweet!"

Through the wire, the puppy licks her fingers
as if they've been sugar-dipped. She's no bigger than
a couple of crumpled Puffs tissues, and seemingly
just as soft and light.

"Would you like to hold her?" asks Germy,
suddenly appearing.

"Thanks, but that's okay . . ." I start to say, only
he already has the cage unlocked. With one deft
motion, he shovels the puppy up and drops her into
Claire's arms.

"Call me when you want to put her back," says
Germy, with a sly smile.

The dog immediately burrows into Claire's
coat, seeking warmth and a vulnerable heart. It
doesn't take her long to find either.

Then it comes. The breathless question I should
have expected all along.

"Dad, can we keep her?"

As a father, I've had lots of practice saying no.
I've withstood tears, tantrums, even desperate little
creatures clinging to my pants cuff. But this is something entirely different. Paul and Claire are wounded.

I can see it in their faces. For once, they are overwhelmed not by simple greed but by genuine need.
They are in love.

One of my most vivid boyhood memories is of
driving home from the animal shelter with my dad.
In a box at my feet was a scraggly puppy of ques-
tionable breed that I had named Inky. He had cost
me $7—the equivalent of 140 returnable soda bot-
tles. I still remember how fulfilling and grown-up it
felt to have something alive depending on me,
something I could shape and love selflessly. It was
my first lesson in life.

Another of my clearest childhood memories is
of an evening 12 years later. I was sitting at the
dinner table, staring blankly at my plate, listening to
my father say grace. At the end, he paused: "And
God bless Inky," he added, his voice breaking. "He
was a good dog." I swallowed hard and blinked
back tears, feeling weak and angry and cheated, but
mostly just powerless. It was my first lesson in death.

I think of all this now as I look at my children
with this tiny white dog, realizing that I'm cornered,

that I can't say no, that she's already theirs. It's an opportunity to create a memory they'll never forget. It's a chance to make them happier than they've ever been. It's my time to bring things full circle and teach them the same lessons I learned.

But it's more than that. To be able to give something that's deeply desired for the right reasons is to fulfill a dream. And that's a father's greatest power. To make a child's fantasy real, to say yes when he expects you to say no, to hold out hope and then satisfy it is to bump up against what it's like to be God. It is joy unequaled.

"Well, how do you like her?" asks Germy, returning.

"She's wonderful!" my kids reply, all starry-eyed.

"I guess we'll take her," say I.

It's a rainy Sunday afternoon a year later, and there's nothing left to do. My wife has gone to work so I'm home alone with the kids—and our dog. "Try to spend some quality time with them," is what she said before she left.

But the remnants of my failed attempts are calf-deep on the family room floor—many of the same toys as before, plus chew chips, rawhide bones, rubber balls, squeaky mice. . . . And that smell? Damn it! She must have had another accident in here.

My children sit amongst it all and say they're bored. Even the dog yawns, as if it's an important point she wants to underscore. That's when I get desperate. That's when I suggest something so foolish, something so dumb, that it makes the kids cheer and the dog's tail thrum.

"Why don't we go look at kittens?"

This time, however, we drive off with identical expectations.

Smarts

HOW A CONSTIPATED BABY PUT ME
IN TOUCH WITH MY INNER EINSTEIN

It's a suppository. Somehow I am supposed to slip this startlingly large red capsule into my squirming baby daughter's porthole. Up until recently, this has been a remarkably prolific orifice, but she's been constipated for 3 days now, and the doctor says this is the best solution. In his office I nodded my head with thankful relief, but what I wanted to say was "Here, you do it."

Being that she's only 4 months old, I have enough trouble getting her diaper on, let alone trying to pinpoint such a specific target without collateral crankiness. And what will happen if I'm successful? That's 3 days worth of formula, mashed yams, and applesauce in there waiting to exit. Are the effects gradual or instantaneous? And why are there six suppositories in the vial? Like bullets in a revolver chamber, are the extras in case I miss?

The thing that continually amazes me about parenting is that you're asked to do it with absolutely no training. You are handed a human being, fragile and priceless, then congratulated, wished well, and told to please exit the birthing suite as soon as possible. Unlike with a new car, there isn't even an owner's manual. It's ironic that everything nowadays comes with a long list of instructions and warnings (in numerous languages) except this. No sir, when it comes to a child, you're on your own.

Here are some suppositories.

Women have an obvious instinct for raising kids. It's what percolates up inside and drives them to have babies in the first place. But men seem to have far less basic knowledge. We can teach them to wrestle, hold a beer bottle, and giggle after a good burp, but that's about it. When it comes to feeding, soothing, and making everything all better, we often don't have a clue—whether they're 16 months or 16 years.

Or at least that's what I thought until I actually started winging it. When faced with any challenge, my first reaction was mild panic. The kid keeps throwing up, throwing tantrums, throwing the car into reverse instead of second—what the hell am I supposed to do?

I know a father whose sweet 3-year-old daughter liked to eat gum off the ground. While he was watching his son play baseball, she'd be scouting under the stands and around the dugout for discarded wads to re-chew. By the end of the game her cheek would be puffed so much, it twisted her guilty smile. It was probably the most disgusting habit I've ever witnessed, made even more horrifying by the fact that her face was so cherubic. Understandably, my buddy would go ballistic. He would yell at her, spank her, punish her. . . . Finally, in desperation, he cut off an inch of her long brown hair and warned that every time he caught her doing this, another inch would go. It worked, but he still worries to this day, at what cost. Had he done the right thing?

You can't depend on parenting books to supply all the answers. Even though there are shelves of them in libraries, they don't contain any chapters on suppositories or gum control. To deal with this, you need inventiveness, luck, and one more very important quality: trust. Not necessarily of doctors, authors, or even your spouse, but of yourself. Regardless of how confused and indecisive you feel at first, *you* know what to do. The trick is simply to listen—to yourself.

This isn't easy. For some reason, people are naturally skeptical of themselves. They feel more comfortable taking orders than making decisions. But man has been around for 300,000 years. Each one of us is a highly evolved creature whose family wouldn't have survived so long if it were inherently flawed. There's already a library inside you, filled with the collective advice of billions of ancestral parents—fathers and mothers who successfully raised sound kids. When you trust yourself, you are really trusting them.

I made an awful lot of mistakes before I realized this. In a well-intentioned attempt to do my absolute best, I was either doing nothing because I was paralyzed with indecision or I was doing something but with nervous tentativeness. I was over-thinking. In retrospect, I was often surprised to realize I'd had the answer all along. I'd just second-guessed myself or let others sway me away from it.

Developing trust in yourself is a big part of growing up—for a child and for an adult. It is the first step toward confidence and, ultimately, success. Now whenever I'm faced with a difficult situation, I try to quiet my mind and determine my initial inclination. I still think through the problem, but in a different way. I do it circuitously. I weigh various options to avoid acting impulsively but always return to the place where I started, listening for the ancestral voice that I know was there advising me when first challenged. And whether I'm acting as a parent, husband, boss, or friend, I've always found— amazingly so—that my initial instinct is the right signal.

I once read a newspaper article in which a famous college basketball coach was asked if intelligence hindered an athlete. Who would he prefer on the foul line with seconds remaining, the crowd screaming, and the score tied? Would he rather a Rhodes scholar or a boy who was struggling in his studies? The coach said there was no question. He would pick the second one—the kid who would shoot like a machine, relying only on his instincts.

And he would be the hero, he would get it done, he would be the emulated one. There's no difference in any crucial situation throughout life. Even if you're well-educated, there are times when it's best to let yourself be dumb, to react the way you've been trained, to turn off your brain and empower your inner animal.

My daughter and I survived the suppository crisis. Of course she wailed and I cursed, but in the end I knew how to dry her tears, make her giggle, and even clean up after all the constipation was dispersed. It made me feel good. It made me feel whole. I can handle anything, I just know.

A FATHER'S HEROES

I am not the kind of man who relies on heroes, or even thinks much about the subject. So as I went about putting together this list, I went instead to fathers who have taught me particularly important lessons. Here are several, none of them truly famous but all of whom have affected me deeply.

TOM CANNON

Before this, I wrote another book called *Wisdom of Our Fathers*. For it, I interviewed 138 wise, old dads and asked them all the big, important questions I should have asked my old man. Of all the guys I talked to, one stands out. His name is Tom Cannon. Despite living in a poor section of Richmond, Virginia, on a meager postal clerk salary, he has managed to give away $100,000 (usually in $1,000 increments) to needy people he hardly knows. His generosity spans 25 years. Cannon, who's 73, exemplifies what fatherhood is all about to me: consistently giving small pieces of yourself even when you don't have the time or the energy. Charity is when you have so much you feel obligated to share. Humanity is when you have so little but you share it anyway.

JOSEPH T. KITA

If the name sounds familiar, that's because it belongs to my father. Most of the time, while I was growing up, he embarrassed me. Quiet, career-minded, unathletic, wife-whipped, he represented everything I didn't want to be. Then he died suddenly of a heart attack at age 61, and I slowly started to realize all he'd done. Patient, hard-working, adept, dedicated, he represented everything I *needed* to be. Every boy's father should be his hero, if not ultimately, then at least briefly when he's young and impressionable. A boy needs to see his own potential; a father, his worth. Heroes aren't always superhuman. Like my dad (and maybe yours), they can be remarkably unexceptional men.

BABA ENG

This man is hardly a hero; he is serving a life sentence for murder. But when it comes to being a father, he taught me something unforgettable. Baba Eng had been a prisoner at Sing Sing for 22 years when a new inmate showed up one day and started staring at him. "Dad?" this convict finally asked.

The man was his son, whom Eng had not seen since his arrest and who was now in prison for armed robbery. "It was the worst moment of my life," said Eng. "Here was my son; he had tried to imitate me." Call it justice: He had ended his son's life the same way he had ended another's. But call it also a lesson: He showed me it's a father's example that has the most impact. Kids may not listen, but they certainly watch. And it's what they see—good and bad—that largely determines who they'll be. Perhaps that is Eng's atonement.

MARK JENKINS

This is a friend of mine, same age, two children, a writer, too. But while I'm sitting behind a desk in Schnecksville, Pennsylvania, he's off climbing Mt. Everest, bicycling across the old Soviet Union, or kayaking to Timbuktu. He is an adventurer, an explorer of niches that others have somehow missed. He has guts, whereas I have dreams. But what I admire most is that he has refused to let fatherhood contain him. This is how he justifies it: "It is pathetically common nowadays for parents to use their kids as an excuse for not pursuing their dreams. Shame on them. The surest way to raise a spineless child is to be a spineless parent." To his credit, his daughters are growing up straight and tall.

JED CLAMPETT

Remember him? He was the father on *The Beverly Hillbillies*. Even after striking it rich and moving west, he managed to keep his family unchanged and intact. Although I'm no oil tycoon, I make a decent buck and can honestly say I have trouble keeping even that amount from corrupting us. My Jethro dreams of a fancy sports car. My Elly May insists she needs a new Sunday dress. And our local Mr. Drysdale keeps reminding me about retirement and that now is the time to invest. Materialism has never been more rampant; happiness has never been more of a commodity. It's reassuring to watch reruns of Jed Clampett today. He reminds me that despite all the pressure, there's a simpler, more satisfying way.

Love

**ON THE SLOW,
DEEP MATURING OF A MAN'S HEART**

My son, Paul, was born with six toes on one foot. Next to his right little piggy was a tiny extra toe—perfectly formed, complete with nail—just dangling there. And on the sides of each hand, at the base of both pinkies, were small fleshy bumps where additional fingers had started to bud. (Later, he'd refer to them as his karate nubbins.)

The nurse pointed these out to my wife and me moments after his birth. It scared me at first, because it made me wonder what else might be amiss. But after he was wiped clean and inspected more closely, she explained that it was a common genetic

condition known as extra digits. He was fine otherwise, and in a few months they could easily be
snipped without scarring.

Nevertheless, I'm ashamed to admit that these
imperfections bothered me. I am obsessive about
the things I create, whether they're books or babies.
I wanted my children to be flawless, but instead
here were misplaced commas in a first edition I
thought had been closely proofread.

I took a week off from work to bring my new
family home. I'll never forget my wife walking care-
fully down the steps to our condominium carrying
Paul. It was the start of a busy new life, and I'd set
aside plenty of time to help us taper in. But once he
was settled in his crib, Paul slept for the next 10
hours. Since our house was already well stocked and
scrubbed, there was nothing for me to do. What I
had anticipated as revolutionary was turning out to
be routine. And when he eventually did awake with
an empty-belly wail, I still wasn't summoned for
anything.

It hurt to see how little I mattered. There was

no decipherable plea for a daddy in his cries, no flash of recognition when he would happen upon me with those new blue eyes. When I held him, he clutched me like anything else that was warm and soft and near. And as a result, inside me was born this fear. After a few days, I started feeling guilty that I wasn't overwhelmed by love for this fresh person. Everyone asked me what it was like being a new father, and I said great, but that wasn't really the case. I was ambivalent, disappointed, and wondering if it was all overrated.

For a long time these feelings embarrassed me. In fact, I've never confessed them before. I guess I was ashamed at my selfishness, at my incapacity for unconditional love, and at the cold fact that I didn't immediately cherish this 8-pound, 3-ounce miracle. But at the same time, I can see now that I learned all I really needed to know about love in those first few days of fatherhood. Even though my son couldn't say a word, he taught me four lasting lessons that are not just applicable to new parents, but to all relationships.

Love needs a sixth toe in order to grow. It's

easy to love something that's flawless. There is no challenge to doing that. But this kind of love is shallow and destined to fade because it demands nothing more of us than appreciation. It is called infatuation. When there's an imperfection, though, some blemish in appearance or a chip in character, then any love that develops will naturally be deeper. That's because it requires maturity and grace to accept, some effort on our part to see past. Imperfections are what make people different, definable, and, ultimately, special.

Love is two hearts sitting around twiddling. Love is 5 percent thrills and 95 percent run-of-the-mill. But this is never evident at first, because that's when most of the excitement occurs. It leads us to expect more than we eventually get, and for many that's a gnawing disappointment. A good test for love is if it can thrive amidst the mundane, whether you can find as much shared satisfaction in living the everyday as you can the extraordinary. If so, then it's true. Remember this: Life is largely routine, and love must carry on in these times, too.

Love requires nothing in return. Many people fall in love not with another person but with the come-to-life dream of somebody actually loving them. It's overwhelming when it happens, and it can take years before the flattery fades and this sad realization is made. But the more genuine the love, the less vital it is to be loved in return. Consider a mother and her baby, a father and his rebellious teen, or a wife and her late husband. Love is spontaneous in its combustion. It is born of itself, wells up, and spreads out. It needs no acknowledgment, no kindling, no tiny validating smile from the depths of a crib. It just is.

Love lacks pick-up. I've never experienced love at first sight. I don't doubt that it exists, but I suspect that one of its major precursors is loneliness. For me, love has always been slow to start. I dated my wife for 7 years before marrying her. I didn't realize how much I loved my father until after he died. And my feelings for my children crept in and then intensified. Like anything else, love needs room to develop and grow. If it starts out too big, if it immediately fills your heart, then there may not be anywhere for it to go.

My son, Paul, is a teenager now. He has pimples, peach fuzz, and a real gift for procrastination. He is holding a standby ticket to puberty that, once punched, will send him into the body of a 6-foot-plus muscle man. But in the interim, he's having a tough time leaving his confident boyhood behind. Suddenly, he is all cowlicks and awkwardness. And even worse, he's sure the girls have noticed it.

My wife pointed all this out to me the other day as we watched him playing basketball with his friends in our driveway. It made me realize that I am witnessing his birth yet again. Only this time, I am different.

Later that night, for no apparent reason, I call Paul aside and tell him I'm proud of him. He just shrugs, because nowadays he's never quite sure what to say. Then I reach out, we shake hands, and I feel those karate nubbins.

Friendship

THE TIME-STOPPING POWER

OF GOOD COMPANIONSHIP

The doorbell rings twice at 6:55 P.M. I answer it to find a tiny girl clutching a huge bedroll and practically vibrating with excitement. It's obvious that she's been waiting for this precise moment since receiving her sleepover invitation 12½ days ago.

"Emily!" my daughter squeals, triggering an outbreak of gleeful hopping. Then they zip past me into the house, leaving the bedroll on the stoop.

During the next 5 minutes, three more eager girls arrive in punctual succession. "Melissa!" "Steph!" "Alyssa!" Soon everyone is hopping and squealing, and I've decided to hold off serving the Coke.

For the rest of the night, the world outside their world ceases to exist. I stand on the periphery, an unnoticed sentry, watching five 9-year-old girls so lost in the delight of being with each other that time is forgotten. When their energy is finally depleted around 2:00 A.M., they huddle together asleep on the family room floor, more secure than if they were clutching favorite blankets or teddy bears. And when the morning comes, they pick at their breakfasts and say they're not hungry, so full are they still on each other's company.

After all her friends depart, my daughter has an exhausted pleasantness about her. The last time I saw her this way she was riding the monorail out of Disney World after a very full day.

"Boy, did we have fun," she sighs. "They're my best friends."

I smile with her, remembering times just like that. When I was little, my best friend Mark lived right across the street. Excitement was hearing the doorbell ring, parting the drapes, and seeing him dawdling there. "Can you play?" he'd say, and instantly we'd be gone—up in trees, deep into fields, out on bikes, down at the corner store—doing so much nothing that it felt like something, until a mother's yell ended our reverie and whistled us home like ragged Border collies. I can still feel the long, slow, honey-luxury of those summer days.

In high school and college, I had almost a dozen best friends. Excitement was hearing a horn beep, parting the drapes, and seeing one of their decrepit cars idling there. "Want to go out?" they'd yell, and instantly we'd be gone—music loud, smoke thick, beer warm, testosterone high—doing so much boasting that it felt like we were something, until a looming curfew or next-day responsibility brought us back to reality. I can still feel the sweet, electric freedom of those wild brother nights.

But I don't feel it anymore. Somehow as I've gotten older, I've lost the knack for friendship—the ability to suspend time and surrender myself like those little girls. There isn't anyone, outside of my immediate family, who gives me that much pure satisfaction to be near. In fact, I'm not even sure the friends I have can genuinely be labeled friends.

Those buddies I mentioned before are still around, but whenever one of us gets wistful enough to organize a reunion, it quickly becomes apparent that what we had can never be recaptured. There are awkward pauses in the conversation now. And it's ulcers rather than laughter that make our stomachs hurt. Instead of enjoying who we're with, we keep remembering who we were.

There are guys at work I'm tight with, but I've learned after leaving previous jobs that these are friends of happenstance. When we no longer share the work, we'll no longer have much to share.

There are neighbors I wave to and gossip with regularly, but I don't really know any of them. If one were to murder his family, I'd probably be the guy next-door quoted in the paper as saying he seemed like such a "nice, quiet man."

And of course, there's my wife. We've been married for 15 years, but no matter how close we are to becoming soul mates, I don't think a woman can ever be a man's best bud. A guy needs someone he can share a wordless beer and a belch with, and feel

understood and totally at ease. He needs someone
he can behave badly around and avoid apology. Too
often, women want men to grow up and act their
age, not realizing that we need to be carefree boys
if we're to truly connect.

The ironic thing about all this is I'm not alone
in my loneliness. I see lots of other men just like me
whose entire lives are career and family. Hanging
out with the guys is a childish, troublesome thing
that interferes with being a good husband, father,
and role model.

My dad spent an hour at the bar in the Roo-
sevelt Democratic Club after work each day, a habit
that my mother continually berated him for. But
after he retired and his children left, the friends he
made there were all he had to fill the emptiness.

At his funeral, there were dutiful relatives,
neighbors, and coworkers, but most of the men
filing by his casket were the ones he'd sat next to
on barstools every day. Their handshakes were the
strongest, their condolences the most sincere—
because each of them now had one less friend,

while all the rest were minus just another acquaintance.

My doorbell rang unexpectedly the other day. It was a "friend" of mine named Weber, who I see occasionally. He asked if I wanted to play pinball, since I have a few old machines, and he held out a six-pack of beer as an enticement to throw away the evening.

I was busy, like I always am, and couldn't really spare the time, but it would have been rude to send him away, so I grudgingly let him in. And a few games became many, and the empties grew to 10. We somehow let that silver ball hypnotize us until the outside world ceased to exist. We high-fived over each high score and punched the air with the knock of every free game. When our energy was finally sapped around 10:00 P.M., we shook our heads like old dogs emerging from a nap, startled at where we'd just been.

"That was fun," I said to Weber. "Let's do it again."

And although a part of me knew we might not, it was enough knowing I still can.

A FATHER'S
ESSENTIAL READING

Here is a sampling of books that have particularly helped me as a father, a man, a human being.

EVER AFTER
BY WILLIAM WHARTON

Simply told, yet deeply sad, this is the true story of every father's nightmare. On August 3, 1988, Wharton's 36-year-old daughter, her husband, and their two babies were killed in a highway crash. It was triggered by field burning, a routine agricultural practice in Oregon, that blanketed the road with dense smoke and caused a 23-car pileup. This book is both a tribute to lives ended too soon and a quest for justice still not met. Reading it kept me up deep into the night, then prompted me to give my sleeping family appreciative hugs.

ALL I REALLY NEED TO KNOW
I LEARNED IN KINDERGARTEN
BY ROBERT FULGHUM

His is the classic father's voice, spinning yarns and giving advice. Fulghum dispenses his wisdom in a philosophical yet humorous sort of way that's simultaneously entertaining and life-altering. This book, and all the subsequent ones from him, showed me how to talk to my kids and how to look for great lessons in little things. But most important, it taught me how to think beyond myself—something a father must constantly do.

THE DIVING BELL AND THE BUTTERFLY BY JEAN-DOMINIQUE BAUBY

This book is amazing not so much for its conception as its execution. The author, a 43-year-old magazine editor, has a debilitating stroke. His mind is lucid (the butterfly), while his body is entirely paralyzed (the diving bell). The only thing he can move is one eyelid, but this doesn't stop him from developing a code of communication with his therapist by which he blinks out the reflections in this book. The most poignant is when his children visit him one Sunday at the hospital, yet he can't touch them, speak to them, or even hold them.

It's sad how many fathers who aren't paralyzed can't
do the same.

THIS BOY'S LIFE
BY TOBIAS WOLFF

There's a feeling afoot nowadays that a father isn't vital to
a family—that a single mother can raise a child just as well
or that even two lesbians can provide all the necessary di-
rection and love. This book, although written a decade ago,
disputes that. It's the funny-sad story of a boy without a respectable male role model. It's a memoir of the fatherless.
Whenever the author gets in trouble, adults ask him who he
thinks he is, what he thinks he's doing, and what he wants
out of life. But he has no answers. In the end, it's easy to
see why.

ANGELA'S ASHES
BY FRANK McCOURT

Strangely reassuring. That's what the father in this book
is. His name is Malachy. He rarely works, often drinks,

usually lies, and eventually runs off, leaving his wife and children to squeak out a living in 1940s Ireland. Yet somehow, the author draws inspiration from him, enough in fact to become a teller of tall tales himself and write this Pulitzer-prize winning memoir of a childhood as filled with misery as it is with miracles. It made me realize that no matter how poor a father I am, it's in a child's nature to try to understand and adopt what little good there is.

IT'S PERFECTLY NORMAL
BY ROBIE HARRIS

Of all the books ever published, I am most grateful for this one. It's an illustrated children's book about sex. Explicit without being pornographic, simple yet remarkably thorough, it helped me broach a subject I may have forever postponed. I know, I know. . . . It's a father's duty to deliver "the talk." But whenever I tried, my kids just rolled their eyes. So I gave them this book, then asked if there were any questions. Not ideal, I realize, but a whole lot better than the alternative.

INSTANT REPLAY
BY JERRY KRAMER

This is the diary of an offensive lineman for the Green Bay Packers. It was published in 1968 and has absolutely nothing to do with fatherhood. But I list it here because my dad gave it to me when I was 9. He was a diehard Packer fan and idolized Coach Vince Lombardi. He wanted me to read it because it exemplified his work ethic. But there was a problem. The book contained hundreds of obscenities. So my father meticulously scratched out each one with a black pen. That was decades ago, and my dad is long dead. But this book remains on my shelf because whenever I open it, I feel safe and protected. His concern, his hope to keep me forever pure, is not only comforting, but it also reminds me of my duty as a dad.

GROW UP!
BY FRANK PITTMAN, M.D.

I can't even guess how many times I've yelled this at my kids over the years. But I could just as easily be yelling it at my-self. We all need to grow up, and here's a straightforward book that can actually help. Pittman is a psychiatrist and family therapist who has listened to unhappy, immature people for 37 years. From this wealth of experience, he writes humorously, compellingly, and insightfully about what it takes for men and women to be happy grown-ups. Become one, and your children might finally start listening to you.

Discipline

My wife and I have been invited to dinner by a childless, older couple who insist that we bring our kids. They live in a small downtown apartment, so there is no place to shoo the children off to, either outside or in. There is also little to occupy them. The only thing the woman can find in her closet is a 5,000-piece jigsaw puzzle of Big Ben. So I take them aside—Paul, 11, and Claire, who just turned 8—and explain how this is someone else's house, how these people obviously aren't accustomed to children, and how both of them are going to have to behave while we're eating dinner.

They nod in grave, intimidated agreement, then sit down and dump all 5,000 puzzle pieces onto the floor. About 5 minutes later, as I'm sipping wine with our hosts in the kitchen, I overhear Claire saying she's bored.

Nonetheless, they stay relatively quiet and don't disrupt us too much, even though the evening lasts nearly 3 hours. I'm proud of them and also, after half a bottle of wine, proud of myself for raising such disciplined, well-mannered kids. As we're saying our goodbyes, the woman tells us once more what a beautiful family we have. Then, in a dismissive, giggly way she adds: "But your kids are too good. Let them be children sometimes."

It takes a while for this offhand remark to catch up with me. We're maybe halfway home, walking pleasantly. A first reaction when someone makes a disparaging comment about your kids is to brand them wrong and inconsiderate. But the more I think about what she said, the more concerned I become that this woman is perceptive.

Many people have told us how well-behaved

Paul and Claire are. Couples our age in similar life-situations have even asked for advice in raising their children. My wife and I have always believed that we're smart parents, that genetics has little to do with being able to take our kids on long trips or to fancy restaurants. We have taught them respect. We have schooled them in self-control. We have told them repeatedly to "Grow up!" And now, I suddenly realize, they have. We've created two tiny adults.

There's a doctor I know who has four sons. Given his occupation, he's accustomed to dispensing orders, writing prescriptions, and having his patients emerge as generally more robust human beings. So naturally, he took this same approach with his boys. He gave them the textbook treatment: a broad-based education, wide-ranging experiences, and lots of cultural entertainment. But one by one, as they grew older and more independent, they spun off: one into drugs, another into alcohol, the third and fourth into petty crime and even pettier women. His Renaissance men became case studies in disappointment.

In retrospect, the problem was obvious. They had grown up in straitjackets, struggling for years against a well-intentioned but suffocating love. When these constraints eased, they squirmed out of their artificial identities and finally started becoming individuals. But this is a lengthy, trial-and-error process. You can make your mistakes as a child, when everyone is forgiving, or you can make them as a young adult, when the world is much less tolerant and even dangerous.

Fortunately, this doctor's sons didn't self-destruct. In fact, they all eventually became the Renaissance men he had originally set out to create. The only thing they needed that he hadn't supplied was the freedom to do it their way—the simple permission to be themselves.

I wonder whether this is my children's destiny. Are they *too* good? Are they too suppressed? Will they spin off some day in search of the person I never permitted them to be? And will they hurt themselves (and us) in the process?

Three years have passed since that dinner

date. Paul is 14, and Claire just turned 11. They are good kids still. No doubt if that woman ever invited us over again, she'd have the same parting observation at evening's end. And although I study my children more closely now, I have yet to notice any bubbling frustration. It could be that it's just too soon. Or it could be that this is inherently them.

One thing has surprised me, though, and that's how fully formed they already are. By the time children reach double digits, I think their basic moral and behavioral systems are largely finished. There's this misconception among parents that we have 18 years to mold our kids. But that's not true. Once you subtract the first few years of life, when they're not fully awake, and then the teen years, when they fall back asleep, you're left with only a short impressionable span. After that, it's just a matter of re-tightening bolts in a frame that has already been built.

So how do you shape them in such a brief time? How do you make a child *good*? I've gradually reached the conclusion that it's not possible. You can only make a child *bad*. When you look at a baby, you see a perfect miniature human being. And as he grows, he stays remarkably so—until we begin our meddling.

A parenting magazine once asked me to write an article listing all the ways that young children are naturally smarter than adults. I thought of nearly a dozen, including: They take naps (it restores energy and creativity), they graze (five or six small daily meals are better than two or three big ones), they never sit still (fidgeting burns calories), they love animals (pets help control stress), they have best friends (strong social bonds extend life), and they exist in the present (a meditative skill known as mindfulness).

All this knowledge is instinctive. Their neural circuits are programmed for a long and healthful life at birth. But then we enter the picture, shaking our fingers and ordering them to wake up, clean their plates, sit still, get away from that stray, stop hanging around with so-and-so, and, for God's sake, start listening to me!

Here's another true story: An obese man, who is ridiculed daily because of his weight, recalled for me the first time he realized he was fat. It was when he was 6 years old, and his grandfather pointedly told him so. Early on, kids don't recognize fatness, blackness, or any other physical characteristic—in themselves or others. They see the interior before the exterior. It's only when they hear their parents doing it that the reversal of perception occurs, and they begin the cruel imitation.

Face it, children learn bad habits from us. Despite our deep affection, we spoil their perfection.

I'm no longer troubled by what that older woman said to me, and I'm not as frightened that my children will turn out badly. It's not that I'm so smug to think my wife and I are perfect parents. It's just that—I've realized, if anything—we've succeeded in being less meddlesome. It's not that we've made our children good through some skillful use of discipline. It's merely that we haven't interfered as much as some others, and that we've been wise enough to trust them.

On our last family vacation, we stayed overnight on a Louisiana plantation. In the evening there was an elegant, candlelight dinner, preceded by cocktails in the library and followed by coffee in the parlor. All night, my kids were surrounded by priceless antiques and, perhaps even more intimidating, judgmental adults. But their behavior was sterling.

Afterward, as we walked across the damp, cricket-thick lawn to our room in one of the outlying buildings, I put my hands on their shoulders and thanked them for being so good.

I felt two simultaneous shrugs, as if they were saying "Aw, come on, Dad. It really wasn't so tough."

And that was both satisfying and reassuring.

They didn't see it as being good. They saw it as just being.

lesson eight

God

**HOW TWO LITTLE KIDS
INTRODUCED ME TO HIM**

It's Holy Saturday, and I've made a big mistake. In an attempt to beat the Easter Sunday crowds, my wife and I have brought our children to evening mass—even snagged good seats in a pew up front. But somehow we forgot that this is one of the most solemn dates in the Catholic faith. It's the day after Jesus was crucified and the night before he rose from the dead. So the ceremony is suitably elaborate. We've been in church for almost 2 hours, and there's no sign yet of a final amen.

To our mortification, 6-year-old Claire is so tired and bored that she's doubled over as if in pain.

She's sitting with her head on her knees, softly sobbing. I've done everything I can—threatened her, held her, bribed her—but her patience is exhausted. Meanwhile, 9-year-old Paul looks like he's about to be sick. The incense is making him pale, sweaty, and nauseous. I look around for a quick escape route, but unfortunately there is none. Not only are we in the middle of the pew, but a procession of chanting priests is blocking the aisle.

By the time we eventually do get out a half-hour later, my wife and I fear we've traumatized our children for life. Somehow in our quest to ensure their salvation, we may have delivered a spiritually lethal dose of frustration.

But, if anything, religion makes you resilient. This I know. I'm a 12-year veteran of Catholic schools, having survived the Latin catechism, 4 years as an altar boy, and a particularly nasty mother superior known only as Fang. She and many others tried to indoctrinate me, and for a while, they succeeded. Until I realized that nuns and priests are humans, too, and that their god isn't the only one.

There are many interpretations. The sole universal truth is that nobody really knows. It's a matter of opinion.

Nonetheless, here I am raising my kids Catholic. Part of the reason is because it's easy. I know what to do. I've already memorized all the rules. But part of it, too, is that I believe one of the chief functions of religion is simply to remind ourselves that we are not God. Even if my kids don't go to church every Sunday, at least they're kneeling and bowing their heads periodically. And ultimately that has to be healthy.

Overall, though, I think children innately know a lot more about God than we give them credit for. In fact, out of all my religion teachers, the best instructors have been my two kids. They've shown me God in a way no adult could. Their evangelism is pure and innocent and honest. In fact, it's ironic that we expend so much effort bringing our children to God when there's every indication they've already found him. Instead of teaching them, we should be letting them teach us—sort of a reverse

Sunday school. Here's what I've learned from watching mine:

God is everywhere in the world. To see him for yourself, just follow a child's wonder. Faith, by definition, is the firm belief in something for which there is no proof. Adults need it in order to accept the existence of God. Children don't. My son, when he was 1, wore a constant comic expression I later dubbed his "stunned-by-life look." Eyes wide, mouth agog, Paul was plainly amazed by all he saw. Each day was a parade of miracles; it's a stage every child experiences. Yet this world they're seeing never changes; only our perception of it does. The proof is always there.

There's no difference between Catholics, Jews, Baptists, Episcopalians, or any other religion. It's all just "church." I did an experiment once. For a couple of months, my wife and I took our kids to different Sunday worships. In the end, they remembered only minor differences: the size of the church, the personality of the preacher, the style of service. But what's really important—the people, their prayers, and their god—all seemed the same to them. The divine defies distinction.

When the collection plate is passed, it's just as thrilling to give 10 cents as it is to give $10. To a child, the amount doesn't matter. It's the act of dropping something into the basket that's rewarding. Once, my daughter impulsively tossed in a picture she had colored. The usher smiled fondly and then, a few pews later, removed it. Claire couldn't understand. The giving is what matters; the gift is insignificant.

If you want God to be your friend, talk to him like one. I tried reading to my kids from the Bible, but they yawned and asked if I could switch to Harry Potter. My wife tried teaching them formal good-night prayers, but they were usually too tired to remember which line came next. They don't understand this language. It's an awkward way to communicate. To get closer to God, simply talk to him like you do to yourself.

No doubt about it, there are guardian angels. Nature is an exquisitely tuned system of checks and balances. So it makes sense that there's a built-in buffer to a child's naive inquisitiveness. Paul got lost when he was 3. We were in a giant home supply store, only I was looking at string trimmers and he became hypnotized by lawn tractors. And just that swiftly, we were separated. Then I heard my name on the public address. He had somehow found the front desk. How could he have known? How else could he have stayed so calm?

There's a reason why it's so tough to sit still and be quiet in church. I get antsy during mass. There are so many things I disagree with, so many opinions I'd like to share, that I dream of one day standing up and delivering my own sermon. Perhaps that's why kids fidget so much in church. They sense what a bureaucracy religion has become and are naturally uncomfortable with it.

God, as visited through religion, isn't a whole lot of fun. Think what would happen to your marriage or relationship if you met in the same place once a week and said exactly the same thing. No wonder so many people lose touch with God.

My kids tell me church is boring. They whine that it isn't any fun. And I can't argue with them. They're right. For proof, just look at the blank faces in the pews around you. We feel love strongest when it is new, when it is nourished by freshness. Boredom is just as poisonous between people as it is between you and God.

There definitely is a God. Even though I go to church less now than before I was a father, my faith in God is greater. I've become less religious but more spiritual. For all the reasons I've listed and more, I've come to realize there's a force at work in this world that's far beyond us. We come from it and we return to it, so it makes sense that children are closest to it. Besides, when I look at my kids and see how perfect they are, it doesn't take a doctorate in religious studies to realize there's no way my wife and I alone could have created something this magnificent.

THE TRANSCENDENT
MOMENTS OF A FATHER

What are the most priceless moments of fatherhood? Every dad would say something different. But the pure joy behind each and every example would be the same. Here are some of my favorites.

TUCKING MY CHILDREN IN

No time is more special between father and child than the few minutes just before bed. I've found that their age doesn't even affect it. Whether they're 15 months or 15 years, they are the warmest, kindest, and most appreciative of beings during that brief period. Use this opportunity for whatever you like: a bedtime story, a prayer, a discussion. It doesn't really matter. The important thing is your being there, your giving them your full attention for perhaps the first time that day. It's a tremendously comforting feeling to be wrapped in the warm blanket of someone's love.

WATCHING MY DAUGHTER PLAY SOCCER

Claire is one of the best players on her team—a forward who's virtually unstoppable. When she gets the ball at midfield and accelerates, no one can catch her. She's a small-caliber blond bullet. When she's on a breakaway, I'm instantly out of my seat, quietly willing her on because I'm so overcome with pride, I can't speak. The other parents think I have a lot of self-control, but inside I'm pretty emotional. There have been times, when the game was on the line, that I almost cried after she scored. I was *so* happy for her. The feeling was *so* pure. What's amazing is that this is only a game of soccer. As she grows, there will be much, much more.

TICKLING THE LITTLE GUYS

My son is especially ticklish under both arms; my daughter, on the bottoms of her feet. I know the exact spots. Whenever I touch either of them there, they become a bundle of giggles. They want me to stop, but not really. I promise I will, but not soon. Their squirming delight delights me, and I laugh almost as hard as they do, until we both collapse on the floor breathless and happy and ready to do it again. Tickling is a marvelous thing. Think about it: In only two fingers, you hold the power to make children laugh whenever you want to. It even works with grown-ups.

PUTTING PRESENTS ON THE ROOF

I got the idea one Christmas Eve to make Santa's visit extra-special. So after my wife and I tucked our toddlers into bed, we stuffed all their presents into garbage bags and put them on the roof. I slipped a note under the tree explaining that Ol' Saint Nick had eaten too many cookies during his early rounds and couldn't fit down our chimney, so the presents were somewhere outside. Naturally, when my kids crept downstairs before dawn on Christmas Day, they were shocked and disappointed. But after reading the note, they ran for their coats and flashlights. They searched everywhere, until my daughter happened to aim her light skyward and it illuminated the bundles on the roof. Her little mouth fell open, and she pointed in speechless awe. I'll never forget it. Looking back at the dozen or so Christmases since, it was our most wondrous one of all.

CHANGING THAT FIRST DIAPER

It was hot, bulging, and tinged with green around the seams. Somehow, I was supposed to remove this thing from my squirming baby boy, clean him, and slap on another. This from a man who gets queasy watching sirloin being ground at the local butcher. I wanted to pinch my nose but knew this was a two-handed job. I wanted to avert my eyes but feared what might happen if I wasn't attentive. How could so much poop come from something so small? But somehow I did it, not just that first time but a thousand thereafter. And I wasn't grossed out. When it comes to your children, no matter how disgusting, disappointing, or besmirched they are now or may ever become, it won't alter your perception. All parents are inoculated against their kids' crap—literally and figuratively. They're blind to their imperfections. This you realize with that first soiled diaper—after you change it, you love them even more.

BEING IMPERSONATED BY MY KIDS

There's no better feeling for a father than to have his little son or daughter say they want to grow up to be just like him. The problem is kids stop being this direct as they get older. Their admiration becomes less obvious. Often you even think you've lost it. But my boy came home from high school the other day with a list of clubs and course electives. "I think I'm going to take creative writing," he said, "and join *The Trumpet* (his school newspaper)." Son of a gun. I guess your influence is always greater than you think.

Quitting

THE PITFALLS AND PAYOFFS
OF PERSEVERANCE

We're driving home from tee-ball, my 6-year-old son and I. It's been another interminable game, this one lasting almost 3 hours. To help you appreciate what a Saturday morning of tee-ball is like, imagine being shackled to a concrete prison floor and having water dripped on your forehead for 20 years. You want to scream, you want it to stop, but you are completely powerless.

In an attempt to make baseball less "developmentally dangerous" for youngsters, the experts have changed the game. Instead of facing real pitchers, the kids hit off stationary tees. Since none of them

have any upper-body strength, rarely does the ball
(it's been rubberized for safety) dribble more than
50 feet. And since all batters must wear full head
protection, they often run to the wrong bag not because they're confused, but simply because they
can't see. In this "softer, friendlier" game, there is no
striking out, no sliding, no spitting, no sexual bias,
no name-calling, not even any scoring. At the end,
when the teams naturally ask "Who won?" the
coaches are instructed to smile and say, "Everyone!"

"Dad," my son asks, tiny glove on his tiny lap.
"Can I quit?"

He has been playing centerfield today, and it's
obvious it didn't make him feel like his hero, Ken
Griffey. The most action he saw came in the fourth
inning when someone spotted him hopping around
and holding himself. "Must you go pee-pee?" the
coach hollered, to which he swallowed hard and
nodded vigorously. Time-out was called while he
sprinted to the port-o-john and back. So I understand what he's feeling as I look over at his baggy
uniform, devoid of even one good dirt stain. Much

of the challenge and fun has been bled out of the game. Just another "safe, wholesome experience" remains.

I want to quit, too. Three hours every Saturday morning and the time spent shuttling him to twice-weekly practices could be used in much more productive ways—by him and me. But I don't immediately tell him this. Instead, I find myself thinking about one time, years ago, when I quit.

I was 24 and pedaling across Switzerland on a bicycle tour. I'd been riding all day, up huge mountains, past storybook scenery, but the beauty had been fading as my fatigue steadily grew. Most of the other cyclists were stronger than me, so I was alone on the road and suffering noticeably. After you've been climbing for hours on a bike, your mind becomes deceitful and you can experience an optical illusion known as false flats. On less-steep inclines, the road ahead appears to flatten and you become expectant of easier pedaling. But that anticipation is never fulfilled. You struggle on, increasingly frustrated at your inability to go faster.

In a village, next to a roadside alpine spring, I finally gave up. When I got off the bike, my thigh muscles locked like Vise-Grips, cramping so tightly that I doubled over in pain. At that precise moment, a black BMW paused momentarily in front of me. I looked up just in time to see two cherry-cheeked kids in lederhosen pointing at me through the rear window and laughing. It's a mental snapshot I'll never forget.

It wasn't very long before our sag wagon appeared. This is the van that sweeps the day's route for stragglers. I put my bike inside and dejectedly climbed in after it. A few miles up the road, we passed Sally and Ethel, two middle-age women who were also in my group. When we beeped the horn, I was further demoralized to see them wave a greeting rather than a plea for help.

Quitting always seems like a good solution when you're being tempted by it. But after the pain, the anger, or whatever it is that made you quit subsides, most of the time you feel worse. You think no one will notice, that you'll be able to slink away, but that rarely happens. Defeat attracts more attention than victory. It's failure that's truly fascinating.

"Dad?" my son asks again. "I don't like tee-ball. It's so boring. Can I quit?"

I want to say yes. Standing in the outfield, trying to catch the wrong kind of flies, isn't teaching him anything. Neither is swinging at a motionless ball. How can you expect a boy to learn to love the game when you deprive him the startling thrill of making genuine contact, of shouting with wide, surprised eyes: "I hit it!" But I still don't tell him this. Instead, I find myself thinking about one more time, quite different, when I quit.

I was working for a newspaper. I'd been there 5 years covering sports and writing features. Just before Thanksgiving, I profiled an outspoken local jeweler named Tommy Van Scoy. He was the area's self-proclaimed "Diamond King," a multifaceted franchiser who took a used-car-salesman approach to hawking rings. During the course of our interviews, he confessed wild aspirations that included becoming governor and eventually president of the

United States. It was a highly entertaining story; my editor told me so. But the publisher killed it because he feared a boycott from other jewelers that would hurt holiday revenue.

I couldn't believe it. I was pissed. His decision went against everything I had been taught in journalism school about the sacrosanct separation of advertising and editorial. Even worse, when I went into his office to argue my point, he treated me like a kid, as if I were a naive college boy with a lot to learn about real-world business. So I quit. Not right then, like I probably should have, but after many weeks of hard thought and realizing that my future there was limited.

Quitting wasn't an escape this time, it was a way of making a point. To walk away on my final day was so sweet, it could never be considered defeat. I didn't hear any derisive laughter at my newsroom farewell, just heartfelt good wishes and slap-back assurances that the right decision had been made—time *would* tell.

"DAD! Are you listening to me?" my son asks

one more time, pounding his mitt for emphasis. "How come you're not answering? I *really* want to quit."

What do you say to a boy of 6? How do you explain perseverance, integrity, and pride when he's sitting there, blowing a bubble, already preoccupied? How do you help him understand that there are two sides to quitting: when you haven't tried and when you've tried too hard; when you're exhausted from moving and when you're weary of not going anywhere; when you're sore from the effort and when you're frustrated by the lack of it; when you've seen what you're made of and when you're still looking.

"No, Paul, I can't let you."

"But why not?" Bubble pops.

"Because that would be the easy way out. You have to see things through to the end."

I wince at these clichés even as I'm speaking them. I feel like I'm missing a magic chance at affecting him. What I really want to say is there's no point to be made here. Your leaving won't make any difference, either to this stupid sport or, more important, to yourself. Quitting without anything to prove is just quitting. There's no growth in that. It teaches you nothing, except how to run. And once done, it forever tempts you, and you will habitually succumb.

That's what I want to say. That's the advice I want to give my only son. But I don't immediately do it, because I'm thinking of something else. About how truly lasting lessons are rarely lectures. About how your example and your inspiration every day is ultimately more important than what you say.

"Let's hit some balls when we get home," I suggest. "You know, the *real* way."

"Can we?" asks Paul, looking up and brightening noticeably.

Time

WHY CHILDREN HAVE SO MUCH
AND ADULTS NEVER HAVE ENOUGH

My daughter is doing her homework, completing a long list of fill-in-the-blank metaphors for her fourth-grade English class. When she finally finishes, she opens my office door and asks if I can check it.

"In a couple minutes, Claire. I'm almost done with this chapter."

"Okay."

These last 5 months have been tough—working full-time and trying to write a book in the few hours that remain. Rising before dawn, staying up late, asking my wife to occupy the kids on weekends. If only there weren't so many interruptions. . . .

"Dad?" her head peeking in again.

"The less you bother me, hon, the quicker I'll be done."

"Okay."

Despite the pressure, it's going pretty well. My editor loved the first few chapters, and if the rest is as good, I should be able to ask for a bigger advance on the next one. It's amazing what you can accomplish in your spare time. All you have to do is prioritize. . . .

"Dad?"

"All right, Claire. Let me take a look at what you have."

Her list of metaphors is impressive:

> *Fast as a jackrabbit*
>
> *Hungry as a bear*
>
> *Slow as mud*

"These are really good, Claire. Very creative. Maybe some day you'll be a writer, too."

She just shrugs.

Soft as a snowflake
Warm as buns
Busy as my dad

I am momentarily stunned.

"What's this last one?"

"Oh, that was easy," says Claire proudly. "I thought of you right away, because you're always in here working."

I dutifully sign my name to the bottom of the sheet.

"Thanks!" says Claire, shutting my office door as she leaves—just like I taught her.

What a way for my daughter to describe me. I guess I've set the wrong priorities. My progress in one project has evidently come at the expense of another. I somehow lost sight of what spare time is made for.

There was an article in the newspaper recently about how parents are working an average of 1,000 more hours annually than the previous generation. That's time directly out of the family: fewer dinners together, shorter vacations, less goofing off in the backyard. It's too early to gauge the impact of this on American kids, but I just got a glimpse of how it's affecting one of mine. Memories of a father preoccupied—a one-word, dagger-of-a-description for a dad not fully there.

This sets me to wondering how much time a child really needs—or for that matter, a spouse, a friend, or even yourself. Is there a magic ratio of minutes devoted to intimacy achieved? How much or, better yet, what kind of time is necessary for a meaningful relationship and a life fully lived? The more I think about it, the more I realize my children have been teaching me. I've just been too busy to apply it.

The first lesson came from my son, Paul, when he was only 2. I was in the front yard (working even then) when he ran up to me and said he had to pee. It was a critical stage for him, recently freed from diapers but still only fitfully aware of the potty. So I was proud to see him recognizing the need and doing a little anticipatory dance, but I was right in the middle of planting a shrub, so I told him to wait a second.

One second later, I got up from the ground and noticed he was soaked.

What I didn't know is that when a child says it's time, _it's time right now._ Whether he wants to eat, sleep, or urinate, he can tolerate only a short delay between urge and fulfillment. Any longer, and there are major repercussions.

Perhaps the reason adults are so cranky is because we're always postponing things. Not that we should pee wherever we please, but maybe we need to heed our instincts more closely, occasionally follow _our_ schedules instead of everyone else's. Imagine how less constipated the world would be if people weren't forever holding something back.

So when the opportunity arises, seize it. When someone in need asks for your time, give it.

Over the years, my kids have also reinforced the fact that time is artificial. They have no concept of it. It's something they must be taught and then continually badgered about. Getting up on time, being ready on time, not wasting time . . . It remains foreign to them even into early adulthood. That's because man's natural state is time-lessness.

"Daddy, what day is today?" my daughter often asks.

"What day is today?" I echo in disbelief. "How can you not know that?"

But then I'll remember vacations past, long lazy stretches of days melting together with the only noticeable rhythm being the beating of my heart. That's how children live every day. That is the way. Keeping track of time only makes us nervous and mournful of its passage.

So whenever possible, ignore time. When someone asks for the time, grin, and say you don't know it.

There's another lesson my children have taught me, and it's perhaps the most important of all. It has to do with making time crawl. Nothing has made me more aware of growing old than watching my kids grow up. And the older I become, the more I catch myself looking back, relying on memories to make me feel young rather than tomorrow's fun. And that's when the days start to speed by. It's like riding in a car. If you turn your head to look at the passing scenery, you'll see only a blur. But if you keep your eyes straight away, it seems as if you'll never get there. That's how children do it. That's how they slow time. They're constantly looking ahead.

"Just 16 more days to my birthday," says Claire.

"Only 122 more days of school left," says Paul.

When you're forever looking forward, there's no time left for regrets. Perhaps that's why death is ultimately peaceful and why religion can be such a comfort in the end. But the anticipation is only half of it. Participation is the rest. The secret to slowing down time is focus, first on something up ahead and then on whatever it is once it arrives.

So when it seems like time is flying, break your routine. Find a dream. Then totally, selflessly, experience it.

A full year has passed since "busy as my dad" made me feel so guilty. During that time I've made a sincere effort to be more available to my kids, to keep my office door as open as possible. I've even scaled back my full-time job, so I can write more books and still have plenty of time to share. So, out of curiosity, I asked my daughter the other day what new metaphor she might apply to me.

"Hmmm," she said, brow furrowed. "I think it would be 'Important as my dad.'"

"Really?" I replied, flattered. "Why is that?"

"Because you wrote a book."

Well, how about that. While I had been worrying about the negligence, she had already moved on to the consequence. She had judged my effort with a child's typical directness. And what I had produced was evidently worth the sacrifice it took. I had become *important*—maybe not to the world, she'll one day realize, but for the moment at least to her blue eyes.

I'd say that was time well spent.

Sex

NO MATTER HOW MUCH YOU KNOW, YOU REALLY KNOW NOTHING

It's Paul's first date—a junior-high semi-formal that's romantically being billed as "A Night under the Stars." He is suitably polished and pressed: blue button-down shirt, khaki pants, and a sweater vest. His casualness belies the fact that we spent almost 3 hours at the mall before making a purchase. When you're 13, it's tough finding clothes that look sharp yet won't draw any attention.

I am serving as chauffeur for the evening. But there have been a few minor complications. Since my wife is working, I've had to bring Claire. With typical little-sister antagonism, she's asking her brother all sorts of embarrassing questions.

"How come you didn't pop that pimple on your nose? It's a big one."

No answer.

"Are you going to try to *kiss* her?"

Still no response.

"Suppose she's really ugly? Do we still have to give her a ride?"

"Dad, could you please tell her to SHUT UP!"

But I must admit I've had that last worry myself. Actually, two worries. The first is that his date will turn out to be a few flowers short of a bouquet. The second, at the complete opposite end of the spectrum, is that she'll be an arresting young vixen already in C-cups. As a father, what do I say in either situation?

"Son, girls aren't supposed to have hair there. . . ."

Or . . .

"Son, do you think you could introduce me to her mother?"

In preparation for this evening, I've tried to

be a responsible dad. I gave the boy an illustrated children's book that explains everything about sex. He took it, closed his door, and emerged a couple of hours later, slightly sweated. He said he didn't have any questions. I was surprised, yet also relieved.

"Did you bring the book?" asks Claire slyly.

"DAD! MAKE HER SHUT UP!"

Fortunately, Paul's date turns out to be perfect. She's cute, bubbly, and, as far as I can tell, still in a training bra. They sit together in the back, a safe distance apart. She talks, he doesn't, and then the dog throws up.

I forgot to mention that in addition to Claire, I also had to bring our puppy. Unsupervised, I trust her even less than my 10-year-old daughter. Evidently, all the excitement and Tommy Hilfiger cologne has been too much for her. Suddenly she gags, and something unidentifiable comes up. The stench pins us wide-eyed to our seats, like an invisible air bag going off. The girl stops chattering. My son coughs. And Claire, in a panic, starts trying to wipe it off. Meanwhile, the dog—happy again—begins lapping it up.

So we finish the trip with windows down and fan on. It's not long before Paul's date resumes talking and some color comes back into his face. Such is the resiliency of young love.

"The puppy wants to give both of you a big kiss!" taunts Claire, holding her out to them as we arrive at the dance.

The young couple gets out fast. I watch them walk away, trying not to think about what they might do. Let them have their night under the stars. I'll drive home and clean the car.

I can remember having some strong sexual feelings when I was Paul's age. One girl in particular named Jennifer twisted me all sorts of ways. I loved her, hated her, adored her, ignored her, and just missed kissing her one luckless night during a game of spin-the-bottle. Does my son feel the same way about this girl?

I honestly don't know. His heart, although partially my own, is a mystery to me and probably forever will be. This sex thing is just as difficult when you're an adult considering it of your children as when you were a child considering it of your parents. In either case you survive by convincing yourself it just doesn't happen.

It reminds me of my first date. It came late, when I was 16. Her name was Cindi. She had just swapped the "y" for an "i" in her name, because it was more "cheerleady." I pulled up in front of her house in my dad's flesh-colored Volkswagen Fastback. She wasn't around, so I laid on the horn. And after a few unanswered minutes, I did it again. I was starting to fear I had the wrong address when her older sister tapped on my window and said if I didn't come in, like a gentleman, she wasn't coming out. It was my first lesson in dating decorum. Was my son feeling just as nervous and awkward with this girl?

He didn't look like he was. He had applied an appropriate amount of Speed Stick, managed to be ready right on time, and seemed remarkably cool whenever I peeked at him in my rearview mirror. But all these rules . . . that book I gave him covered the core stuff, but everything that surrounds it is what's really tough. Sometimes I think kids have sex just because they get frustrated with all the rest. In our complex society, it's become the easy thing to do.

It makes me think about the first time I touched a girl. Her name was Bridgette, a senior varsity cheerleader. We were at a drive-in movie, making out in the back seat, when she slipped my hand beneath her bra and started moaning. It was a dream come true. But there was one problem. Unlike in the *Playboy*s I'd seen, she didn't have any breasts. In fact, she didn't even have any bumps. I was totally befuddled. These nipple things must really be something special. Will my son be just as naive when his time comes?

I can't tell. He certainly seems like he has it together. I mean, he's had health classes in school, and I gave him that book. But come to think of it, I didn't see anything in there about young breast-less women, fake orgasms, or what you're supposed to say when it's not good for you. Such situations you have to muddle through. Unfortunately, that's still how we teach love around here. The most advanced of subjects has a curriculum that's never been clear.

Like the first time I had sex. It was with a girl named Maria, and it was unintentionally intentional, I guess. Lying together in bed, tender and warm, it seemed like the next natural step. But the following morning while I was driving her home, she was uncharacteristically quiet, scared by what we had done. I held her hand, reaffirmed my love, and said there was nothing to be ashamed of. Is my son aware that compassion should follow passion, that sex is a touching of souls as much as of bodies?

I honestly don't know. But I'm starting to see that the reason I don't understand my son is because, when it comes to sex and love, I still don't understand myself. Why couldn't I just come out and tell Jennifer that I liked her? Why had I felt so uncomfortable treating Cindi like the little lady she already was? Why didn't I just take my hand out of Bridgette's bra and ask her, right then, how that could feel so good? And why, amidst Maria's regrets, didn't I confess how scared I was too?

Even though it has been years since these experiences, I still don't have any answers. And without them, I'll never be able to explain things to Paul. I'm ashamed to admit that after all this time, I don't understand sex any better. But maybe we were never meant to. Maybe if we understood all the dynamics between a man and a woman, it would cease being so mysterious and wonderful. Maybe not being able to totally comprehend it is what makes it so fascinating and marvelous. Like the cosmos, sex is so transcendent, so big, that we'll never be able to wrap our arms around it. So maybe I shouldn't feel guilty about that. Maybe it's enough for us to stand alongside each other in wordless awe, whether we're father and son or husband and wife, and admit that part of the thrill, part of what we call love, is dependent upon never quite being able to explain it all.

THE MUSIC OF FATHERHOOD

There are songs and sounds that are inextricably linked to being a father. Here are several, from my vantage point.

THE NATIONAL ANTHEM

Whenever it played, my dad would stand and I would mimic him—back straight, head high, hand over heart, expression proud. What every man wants in a country is also what every boy wants in a father.

SNORING

I'd wake up suddenly in the dark—a frightened boy alone with his nightmare. Then I'd hear my father snoring in the next room and instantly know that I had had a bad dream, that everything was okay, and that as long as he could sleep so soundly, I was safe. From what my family tells me, I am carrying on the tradition.

"THE BEER BARREL POLKA"

Every summer Sunday, my father would listen to polka music on the radio—the "Jolly Joe Timmer Show." He'd sit on the patio reading the paper, sipping a beer, and tapping his foot. It was the sound of our Polish heritage and his youth. Whenever I happen across it now, I think of him. I don't like it any better, but I know it's my duty not to forget it.

"CLAIR"

Written by Gilbert O'Sullivan in 1972, this is a song about a beguiling little girl that ends with her mischievous giggle. Sixteen years after it was a hit, I inexplicably heard it again in a dream. Nine months later, it's what we named our baby daughter. And as promised, she's made our life lyrical.

"CAT'S IN THE CRADLE"

A busy father and a hopeful young son. These are the only characters in this classic Harry Chapin song. Each verse spotlights a different time in their relationship—the boy always asking, the father usually postponing—until at the end their disappointments are reversed. A busy son and a hopeful old father. "He'd grown up just like me," is the chorus lament. "My boy was just like me. . . ."

"THE BOY IN THE BUBBLE"

Thank goodness for this song by Paul Simon. When my son was a cranky baby, it would instantly calm him. I'd cradle him in my arms in front of the stereo, turn up the volume, and rock him along to the chorus: "Don't cry baby, don't cry, don't cry. . . ." He's a teenager now. How I wish there was similar music that could settle him.

GRACE

It's a father's job to say it reverently before every meal: "Bless this food which we are about to receive from thy bounty through Christ our Lord, amen." I must have heard my dad deliver it 10,000 times. He'd speak in a deep monotone, making all the words flow together as if they were one. To this day, it remains my favorite note of thankfulness.

"SUNRISE, SUNSET"

I can't listen to this song at a wedding without getting choked up. It captures the ebb and flow of life so well, especially a father's joy and sadness. Whenever I hear it, I dream of one day walking my little girl down some church aisle and handing her over to the man of her dreams. I'll cry then, I know, and shake my head at how the days have flown.

Trust

WHAT A MIDNIGHT INTRUDER

SCARED ME INTO REALIZING

The telephone is ringing at 2:30 A.M. I groan and wait for the answering machine to pick up. One ring, two rings, the start of three, then nothing. Only the rain falling heavily outside. Whoever it was has hung up. I roll over and bunch the pillow, cursing.

My cobwebbed mind drifts. Perhaps my mother is sick—hand clutching her chest, night sweats thick, unable to decide what to do. Doesn't she know to dial 911? I'm too far away to drive there in time . . . especially in this weather. . . . Tossing, turning . . .

The phone is ringing again. It's 2:40 A.M. I'm more awake now but still too tired to throw aside the covers and run to the kitchen to answer it. One ring, two rings, the start of three, then nothing.

I bet it's one of my son's friends, dialing and smiling at his disturbing joke. I stare into the dark, wishing for caller ID so I could torment the little jerk every night for the next month. I'll call the phone company tomorrow and order it. . . .

Then, as I start to doze once more, I hear it— something I cannot ignore. *Someone is at the front door.* There's the jiggle of an unpracticed hand at the lock—the focused yet fumbling sound of a stranger trying to figure it out. And instantly, I'm wide-eyed and alert.

The red seconds on the bedside clock pass like minutes. I lay there, listening and thinking. It can't be my wife because I heard her come home from work hours before. It can't be my kids because I know they're tucked safely away upstairs. And it can't be the storm because wind-blown branches don't make that sound.

With no possibilities left, I force myself to get up and investigate. I'd been working in my den late last night and had grown so tired I'd fallen asleep on the cot that's there. So I am next to the entry hall, no more than 10 feet from the front door. I peek through the tall, narrow window that looks out on the stoop and see a cloaked figure—wet and wild-haired. A hand is on the doorknob, and it's starting to turn.

You're probably thinking that all this detail is purely for drama. But that's not true. When you're frightened and roiling with adrenaline, this is the way you see things. It's a sort of slow-moving, natural night vision. I am scared stiff, but at the same strange time, I am also scared calm.

Suddenly, the door swings open, rain spattering in, and the figure turns my way and screams. I jump back, at the same time realizing that I know this face, this voice, this tan raincoat. It's my next-door neighbor, Mary Ellen.

"Oh my God!" she stutters, her face white and hands all aflutter.

"What are you doing?" I stammer back, relieved but also peeved at finding her here.

"The alarm company. They called and said there was a problem. I didn't know if you were home, so I thought I'd better check."

And we stand there, quiet at last. The racing hearts, the trembling, all becoming overwhelming. I put my hand against the wall, feeling unexpectedly weak despite my relief.

I know what must have happened. The alarm company, detecting a malfunction, first called here. When there was no answer, it dialed the next emergency number, which was Mary Ellen's. Then when she couldn't rouse us (the second phone call), she grabbed the spare keys we'd given her and came over herself. Fortunately, neither one of us was carrying a baseball bat or, worse yet, a gun.

"Thanks," I say, giving her shoulder a reassuring squeeze. "I'm really sorry about this."

And I close the door, double-check the lock, and take one long, deep breath to steady myself. If I were a drinking man, this would be the time for a

tumbler of scotch. But instead I walk upstairs to
where my family is. Unbelievably, they are still
sleeping. In fact, their sheets are so smooth I can tell
they've barely moved. Paul is snoring, mouth open,
gangly limbs splayed at reckless angles. Claire is
peaceful, lips closed, arms around Snuffles, her favorite stuffed animal. I shake my head and kiss them
both. They rest in total trust.

Unable to sleep for the remainder of the
night, I'm in the living room reading when Claire
comes downstairs the following morning. She's
wrapped in flannel and the fuzziness of awakening.
"Good morning, Daddy," she says, stretching.
"I slept really good. Do we have anything for
breakfast?"

I can still remember falling asleep in my father's car when I was a boy about her age. We'd be
driving somewhere far, and he'd notice my heavy
eyes. "Go ahead, take a nap," he'd say, and I'd slouch
in the seat and instantly drift away. I knew he'd take
care of me, keep me safe, and get me there.

I can still recall almost getting hit by lightning

when I was a fearless young teen. My father and I were playing bean bags in our backyard when there was a white flash, a thunderous boom, and a palpable sizzle. I ran to him, screaming, and hugged him tighter than I ever had. I did it without thinking; it was instinct. And he stood firm, squeezed me back, and said, "Everything's okay."

And it was.

Such peace, such reassurance, such trust I am no longer capable of. Although I try to appear otherwise, I have this constant, unsettling watchfulness inside. I can't fall asleep in cars anymore. Whether it's my wife driving or a friend, I can't close my eyes and feel that same security. I'm scared of thunderstorms, too, and being caught outside under a blackening sky. I am the tallest oak now, exposed and vulnerable. And I'm increasingly suspicious of people, skeptical that there's anyone left who is completely selfless.

All this started to happen when I became a father, a faithful guardian of two innocent souls. And it grew worse when I lost my dad, and I realized there was no longer anyone I could run to. This is the evolution of man—from one who reaches out for comfort to one who is reached out to. It's a subtle shift, but it makes for profound change. Suddenly, it's *you* who sleeps with one eye open, *you* who investigates those strange night sounds, *you* who must swallow the fear and say, "Everything's okay," convincingly and clear.

It's a responsibility that never leaves. But for all its demands, there are substantial rewards. Looking at my daughter now, all rested and warm, I feel a tremendous sense of satisfaction, like I've been her roof in this storm. Even though she doesn't appreciate it now, I know that she will one day, when the phone rings at 2:30 A.M. and it's her duty to answer it, or when there's a jiggle at the lock and she's the only one who hears. Then she'll remember, then she'll realize, then she'll grow.

Life is a sequence of roles, a process of ever-expanding responsibility. We fall into the next, we acquire more, but it's always without fully comprehending. Then something happens to show us how far we've come and how much we're depended upon. It's a frightening moment. It awakens us to our vulnerability. But it does something else, ultimately. It makes us realize that we're needed, that without us others couldn't sleep or live so soundly, and that is the most gratifying feeling of all.

Death

**HOW A SLEEPING BEAUTY
AWAKENED ME**

Early one morning while my 8-year-old daughter Claire is sleeping, I walk softly into her bedroom. Her thick, curly, blond hair lies wildly across the pillow, and I'm pleased to see that she's still being guarded by her army of stuffed animals. So deep is her sleep, it barely seems like she's breathing and, in retrospect, maybe that's what made me check.

I put my hand on her smooth, warm cheek and a thumb lightly over one eye. Then, ever so gently, I lift her eyelid and look to see what's inside.

But there's nothing there, except a faraway vacant stare.

And suddenly I'm thinking of another morning, years ago, when I walked softly into my father's bedroom and saw the same gaze. His thin, gray hair was matted from the heart attack he'd suffered that night, but I was pleased to see that watching over him was a wedding day photo of his wife. I put my hand on his rough, cold cheek and used my thumb to close his eyes. Then I kissed his forehead, whispered "I love you," and said goodbye.

You expect parents to die. That is the natural order of things. The inevitability of it helps temper the grief. But no parent expects to bury a child. That is unnatural. That is something beyond sorrow.

My daughter is fine, but because I've peeled back the veneer of unconsciousness, because I've never seen her eyes devoid of glimmer and dance, I am shaken. She is here but somewhere else. She is breathing, but slowly. She is alive, but out of reach.

I know an old man who lost two children to influenza "48½ years ago." He buried each one, by hand, on his Iowa farm. Imagine that. Digging holes in the earth, shovel by shovel, in which to lay your kids. Although it happened almost half a century ago, he said he still thinks about those children every day. Nothing in his hard life hurt more. No work ever made him ache so much. And although the holes in the ground were filled, the one in his heart was not.

I know a young couple who lost a baby girl about 10 years ago. She was born prematurely and lived only a few weeks, but there was still a funeral. Imagine that. Tucking your child into a little white coffin as if it was a crib, but instead of winding up a mobile, they make you close the lid. Although this couple went on to have two healthy kids, they eventually separated. The memory of their failure was too great. That tiny person had taken away a piece of their souls that could never be replaced.

As I cup my sleeping daughter's head in my hand and look into her eye, I think about what it would be like if she died. And the thought both terrifies and embarrasses me. I have crossed into a place where parents aren't supposed to go. I am considering the blackest of possibilities. Part of me wants to leave her room and never think about this again—never confess to anyone what I've done. But part of me also wants to stay, because there is newfound appreciation flooding into me.

Much of the hurt from my father's death stemmed from never having anticipated it. Although I knew he would pass away someday, I never thought it would be *that* day. He was 61, healthy, an ex-Marine. At the time, in my mind, "father" and "forever" were still synonymous. And that's why his sudden death left me with so many gnawing regrets. If only I'd attended a rehearsal. If only I'd given myself a warning. If only I'd realized how fragile he was despite how strong he looked, I wouldn't have been left with so much emptiness.

I make this mistake with people all the time and especially, I see now, with Claire. Because I'm afraid and embarrassed to consider her departure, I often take her for granted and let our time together become habitual. When she complains that she's bored, I shouldn't get upset. Instead, I should welcome the reminder and be thankful for her perceptiveness.

Later in life, the cliché parents' lament is that they don't know where all the time with their children went. Grown before you know it. Gone in the blink of an eye. If there was just some way to slow it down, to suspend the specialness, to accumulate keepsakes more meaningful than videotape and photographs.

I know how to do this now. You have to scare yourself. You have to realize that this child you're touching has a grasp on life that's as tenuous as puffs on a dandelion. And you have to remind yourself regularly of this. You have to look her in the eye every now and then when she's not there. You have to think about holes in the ground and little white coffins.

I know it sounds gruesome. I know it makes you squirm. But I do it now with all the valuable people in my life. I've found that the moment I start thinking about losing someone I love, I immediately win them back.

The light is brightening through Claire's window, and it's time for me to leave for work. I rearrange the covers around her and rescue a fallen stuffed animal or two. A parting that would normally take seconds has lasted minutes today. But rather than feeling rushed, I feel strangely blessed. By being given a glimpse of life *without*, I've suddenly become more appreciative of life *with*.

And once again I'm remembering that other bedroom, years ago, where I kissed a forehead, whispered "I love you," and said an unanswered goodbye.

I do the same thing to my daughter now, only this time there's a sigh, a gentle rustling, and, ever so softly from deep within the sheets, a single squeak.

"Bye, Daddy," she says.

"Bye, Precious," say I.

WORDS THAT MOVE
A FATHER

Here is a healthy dosage of parenting common sense and inspiration that I have picked up along the way.

"I have three simple rules for dealing with kids. One: Listen to them and look at them while you're doing it, because most adults don't. Two: If you have a choice between telling the truth and being kind, be kind. Three: Let them know, in no uncertain terms, that if they violate the rules, there will be consequences."

—KEVIN MILLER,
a friend of mine who also happens
to be a middle-school teacher

"Every son has a busy father and doesn't get the attention he deserves."

—F. LEE BAILEY,
the famous defense attorney

"I was coaching Little League, and there was this 9-year-old named Josh, the son of a single mom. He was a big kid but he couldn't hit the ball, and he was ashamed. So I started working with him one-on-one.

"The next to last game of the year, Josh comes up to

bat. The week before he had popped up to the pitcher with the bases loaded. He felt terrible. Anyway, he gets up, and he just creams the ball. I mean, he creams it. He starts running toward first and down toward second. I'm on third, coaching the base, and when he sees me waving him home, he looks at me—I'll never forget it as long as I live—and there are tears in his eyes. He ran home, jumped in the air, and landed with both feet on the plate. The whole dugout cleared out to hug him.

"Nothing replaces that. Nothing in the world. I mean, to literally change a kid. That was the best time of my life."

—JAMES CAAN,
the actor, who stepped away
from a lucrative film career
for 6 years to coach his sons

"Rule No. 111: A man in a minivan is half a man."

—*ESQUIRE* MAGAZINE (SEPTEMBER 1999),
reprinted here only because it pisses me off.
A man in a minivan is *twice* a man.

"Love is a combination of admiration, respect, and passion. If you have one of these going (in a marriage), that's about par *for the course. If you have two, you aren't quite world-class, but you're close. If you have all three, then you don't need to die; you're already in heaven."*

—WILLIAM WHARTON,
one of my favorite authors,
when asked by a troubled daughter
how to tell when it's time to divorce.
If my children ever ask me for advice that big,
I hope I can be half as brilliant.

"When I was a boy of 14, my father was so ignorant I could hardly stand to have the man around. But when I got to be 21, I was astounded at how much the old man had learned in just 7 years."

—MARK TWAIN,
as delightfully insightful as usual

"The first half of our lives is ruined by our parents and the second half by our children."

—CLARENCE DARROW,
the lawyer who defended
the teaching of Darwinism in a famous
1920s court case. I like the pessimism.

Words That Move a Father

"*There are few things as seemingly untouched by the real world as a child asleep.*"

—JOHN IRVING,
author.
I only wish I could keep them that way.

"*Instead of being a father, which is often a biological accident, become a dad. Children in the South often refer to their male parent as Daddy. To me, that always seemed to hold out more possibility for affection, nurturing, and sharing than just being someone's father.*"

—NICK RATH,
a fellow who's called Daddy by 3 biological,
6 adopted, and 18 foster children

"*In three words I can sum up everything I've learned about life: It goes on.*"

—ROBERT FROST,
poet

"*What I tell my kids is that I may give you lots of beautiful words, but watch my life. There's a difference between fine words and fine living, what people say and what people do. My kids have said terrible things to me—that I'm old, I'm stupid, or that they hate me. But when I look at them, I see that there are a lot of my values that they continue to live out. Something stuck. And that comes through the example I give every day."*

—ROBERT FULGHUM,
author and the wisest living man I know

"A father is someone who carries pictures where his money used to be."

—SOURCE UNKNOWN.
Or maybe it's because he realizes
there are more important things.

"Sometimes, looking at (my parents), I wanted to bash their heads with a tire iron. Not to kill them, just to wake them up."

—KATHERINE DUNN,
writer. You know what? I'm 40,
my mother is 65, and I still
get the urge to do this.

"Strive as valiantly to work and succeed with your family as you do with your career."

—PHIL MULKEY,
a former Olympian
who knows a lot about dedication

Words That Move a Father

"Sure I love my parents, but they're going through this phase of thinking I'm too young to make my own decisions about anything. I guess this is what usually happens to parents. When you're born, they have to do your thinking for you, and they get into the habit. Then they keep trying to think for you your entire life."

—FLORENCE PATTY HEIDE.
No idea who she is,
but she really nailed it here.
The worst mistake a father can make
is not letting his babies grow up.

"Sex is one of the greatest joys on earth. It's like Christmas. But it can be the same as having Christmas every day of the year if one becomes promiscuous. There won't be any thrill left."

—WILLIAM WHARTON.
When it came time to give
his teenage daughter "the talk,"
this is what he told her.

"I love (my parents), but what if I could actually talk to them? I mean what if they had some answers? Or would that just be too weird?"

—PAUL RUDNICK,
playwright.
And, yes, that would be too weird.

"Any fool with a dick can make a baby, but it takes a real man to raise his children."

—LAURENCE FISHBURNE,
in the movie *Boyz n the Hood*.
Ain't that the truth.

"I've found that the best way to give advice to my children is to find out what they want to do and then advise them to do it."

—HARRY TRUMAN.
A scheme so good, it also got him elected president.

"Don't try to make your children into what you want them to be or what you weren't. Educate them, most of all. Make education available to them as long as they want it, anyway they want it."

—JOHN D. CAHILL,
a very smart man

Words That Move a Father

"Only 1 in 10 children experiences relief when his or her parents divorce. Divorce is a very different experience for children and adults, because the children lose something that is fundamental to their development—the family structure."

—JUDITH WALLERSTEIN and
SANDRA BLAKESLEE,
two Ph.D.'s

"Introduce your children to sports, but always pull back after they get the hang of it."

—JIM LAW,
a gifted coach

"You know you've grown up when you would rather have Christmas at your own home with your own kids, than go off to your parents' house."

—WILLIAM WHARTON,
one last time.
I don't know about you,
but I don't go anywhere.

Worth

HOW TO PICK YOURSELF UP

WHEN A SON LETS YOU DOWN

I drop my daughter off at the athletic fields behind our local high school. She's in a soccer clinic this morning, and since it's only supposed to last an hour, I park nearby to wait and watch. The boys' varsity and JV teams are warming up, dribbling balls and taking shots. They're wearing their uniforms, looking sharp. It's their day to be stars and show the little ones how it's done.

That's when I realize that I know some of these guys. My son, Paul, used to play soccer with them. That's Chris from up the street. Man, is he getting tall. And there's Alex from the travel team, still working his magic with the ball. And that must be Ryan. Look at the muscles on him. And there's Evan in goal. His father must be proud.

I am surprised: first, at how grown-up they all appear. They are boys no longer. They are young men, role models even. I hadn't placed my son in that category yet. To me, he's still Osh Kosh coveralls and a cocked baseball hat. I guess because I see him every day, I haven't noticed how much he's changing.

But more unsettling than that is the fact that his former teammates are here and he is not. For the first time in my nearly 15 years as a father, I have a very painful thought: *My son is not good enough.*

This realization makes me immediately sad, as if I'd just hung up the phone after learning of a friend's death. I had always believed my boy had unlimited capabilities, that he could achieve anything he wanted, that he was already more perfect than I could ever be. And I know he would have wanted *this*. He would have loved to be wearing that uniform, playing the role of high-school stud, teaching his best moves to kids smaller than himself. Indeed, he had tried, but he had gotten cut.

My son, he wasn't good enough.

Paul has never disappointed me. Even when he brought home poor grades or discipline slips, I knew that with the proper admonishment and encouragement he would eventually correct the problems. And he has. He's shown me the ability to overcome a deficiency, and I always took that as a sign of budding character and destined success.

But this is different. His not making the team wasn't due to just a few mistakes. Even if he had become obsessed with soccer and practiced it until the backyard was bare in spots, I don't think he ever would have been good enough. You can only polish basic skill so much. What he lacked was ample ability.

Reincarnation isn't something I have a lot of faith in, but some believers preach a theory I find interesting. It holds that you keep coming back in subsequent lives until you get it right, each time learning from your mistakes, building upon your strengths, until you're eventually the best person you can be. And that is when reincarnation ends. That is heaven.

Every father feels himself reincarnated as his son. This little boy looks like you, talks like you, acts like you, in fact, wants to be you. For me, one of the most rewarding parts of having a son is the opportunity to watch myself grow up. This is what I must have been like at that age, this is myself in a mirror that looks back decades. There's no end to the wonder of that.

But there's another feeling, too—the thrill of holding in your arms not just a son, but a second chance. You hug it close to your heart, believing you're loving a boy but actually cherishing something else. Here is the possibility to remedy every regret, to realize all those unrealized dreams, to rewind life and play it again, only at higher quality. It's a tremendously fulfilling and dangerous undertaking. Do it right and your pride will be unequaled. But do it wrong and your disappointment can be eternal.

I never played soccer when I was young, but I was on baseball and basketball teams. A few times I experienced athletic glory, pitching a shutout, scoring 18 points. It was just enough of a taste to wish I had gotten a bigger swallow. So I naturally pushed my son that way. Only he never caught on in baseball, and he just wasn't big enough for basketball. Now even soccer, the one sport he had been respectable at, has left him behind. Maybe I feel so sad because a dream of mine has just died.

One thing children don't immediately have is expectations for themselves. When they participate in something new, they're focused on the present, not the future. They're on the inside, doing, not on the outside, evaluating. When they show an ongoing interest, that's when we interfere, telling them they can do it this way and that—overwhelming them with possibilities. We excite them. We instill hope. We give them our goals. Then, when ultimately they get measured and fall short, we realize we've unwittingly taught them disappointment. Most times when children feel inadequate, it's not because they think they've failed; it's because they notice they've failed us.

My son isn't as talented at soccer as Chris or Alex or Ryan. He doesn't have one of those sharp-looking uniforms. While these young men are out being role models, he's probably at home watching music videos. I have to admit it hurts. I have to confess that I wouldn't mind being Evan's dad, standing on the sidelines right now, taking photographs. But that's not my son's reality; it's me again, dreaming.

Like everyone else, his capabilities are limited. What he can achieve does have boundaries. There is no son anywhere who can be as perfect as his dad plans.

I had a 70-year-old father tell me this: "At first, men tend to love their kids conditionally because that's the kind of world we live in, a place where things are always being measured. But with age, you come to love your kids more like their mother always did, unconditionally. You gradually accept them for who they are, you stop trying to influence them, and you just support them."

Maybe I should be proud that my son isn't good enough. Maybe I should be proud that he has withstood being judged. Maybe I should be proud that he tried and failed rather than failed to try. Maybe I should be proud that he's different, that he's on his way to becoming his own man, unique and free. Maybe I should be proud that he isn't turning out just like me.

Wonder

**THE FACE THAT LAUNCHED
A THOUSAND TRIPS**

I have just passed through the gates of the Magic Kingdom, paying $775 for "5-Day Super Duper World Hopper" tickets for me, my wife, my mother, and two children. It is Day One of our 2-week Disney World vacation, and I'm standing on Main Street feeling like I've just had my pocket picked. Nearly a thousand dollars for park admission, and we haven't even encountered our first souvenir stand or soft-drink concession.

Freshly determined to see and ride everything at least twice, I turn around to hurry my family on, but stop at the sight of my kids' faces. Eight-year-old Paul and 5-year-old Claire are standing there, frozen in fascination. Their little heads are tilted skyward toward Cinderella's castle, and their mouths are open wide enough to almost see their tonsils. They are in heaven's lobby, eyes big with wonder, temporarily convinced that everything imaginable is possible.

But before I can grab my camera, the trance passes and they are running toward me—Claire already saying that she's a little thirsty. I take their hands, but I let them lead. My job is done; now it's their turn to show me how to have fun. So we squeal through Mr. Toad's Wild Ride, with both of them believing they can actually drive. We duck under cannonballs on Pirates of the Caribbean, and during the Jungle Cruise, we narrowly avoid being eaten. They cover their eyes with parted fingers in the Haunted House and scream with delight on Splash Mountain when we unexpectedly get doused. And late each night when I tuck them into bed, it's with the theme from It's a Small World playing in their heads.

But despite all this excitement, I never again see a look on their faces quite like that first one. I don't need a photo to remember that moment; their expression will never leave me. That's because it represents everything a father is supposed to provide—amazement, opportunity, and reassurance that magic still exists in the world. In retrospect, it was a bargain at $775.

I once met a veteran attorney and politician who said his greatest joy was closing the door on all of life's charades and turning on the Discovery Channel. He told me that no matter how cynical he got during the day, he knew there would always be something on to amaze him. Whether it was rare footage of poison dart frogs in the rain forest or new sonar blips from deep in Loch Ness, it never failed to restore his confidence in a grand plan, bolster his belief in the intelligence of man, and remind him of the many miracles that still exist. To him, the three most important words in life were not "I love you" or even "I am sorry," but rather "How 'bout that"—mumbled privately.

In the years since, spurred by that fleeting expression of wonder, I've taken my children on many adventures. I saw the look again in Ireland when, after two weeks of bicycling through fog and soft rain, the sun emerged and everything was suddenly crystal green. I noticed it once more while rafting Idaho's Snake River, when our guide had them listen to the hungry, faraway thunder of the first big rapid. I watched it settle upon my son at a small restaurant in southern France when, on his 12th birthday, the chef's best was ceremoniously set before him. And I saw it temporarily transform my daughter, when in the wilds of British Columbia we came upon a fresh bear track twice as big as her head.

But don't get the wrong impression. To evoke this look, you don't have to travel far. In fact, I've often witnessed it in my backyard. Like when you pick a plump, green caterpillar off a sprig of parsley, put it in a jar, and a week or two later have a black-and-yellow butterfly. Or when you build a miniature house, hang it in a tree, and, come spring, have it stuffed with chirping baby birds and all their debris. When little things like this have happened, I've seen that exact same expression. My children stare at me and ask, "How can this be?"

This look of wonder has become like a drug to me. When it appears, I know that I'm doing my job as a parent, that I am introducing them well to the world. It gives me such an incredible satisfied high—it's still so completely wondrous to me—*I* feel like a kid on Main Street in Disney World.

But as my children grow, it's becoming more difficult to inspire them. Perhaps it's a sign that my job as parent-guide is ending. Soon, it'll be up to them to travel to places and discover things that satisfy their own unique sense of wonder. But at least I've taught them to look for it and to believe that it exists. And I guess it's also a signal to me that since I no longer have little children to bring wonder to my life, I better start looking for it elsewhere.

Most of us sleepwalk through adulthood, eventually coating everything with a thin, seen-it-all-before veneer that keeps us safe and pleasantly bored. We need to wake up every now and then, to stand in momentary suspended awe before some piece of creation. It's not hard. In fact, I've started using a few simple tricks. Like I never go to the same place twice on vacation. A getaway should be just that: an escape from the familiar, a restoration. Also, whenever I grow tired of walking, running, or cycling the same route near my home, I simply do it in reverse. Try it; you'll be amazed at what you've missed. And finally, I talk to people, not about the weather or sports or what's on TV, but about the things in life that matter, the thoughts and experiences that make us wonder about ourselves.

"Come quick! Come quick!" my children whisper to me. "Look what we've found." And in the shallows of the lake alongside where we're camped are two huge snapping turtles engaged in a curious dance. I'm momentarily frozen in fascination, watching them mate. Until, out of the corner of my eye, I notice my children watching me. I see the pride of discovery and the joy of having shared it in their faces, and I know right then that they'll turn out all right.